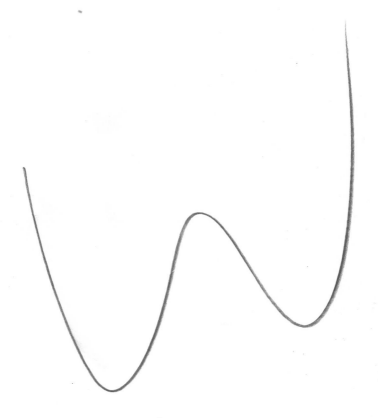

Spin Cycle Stop

A practical handbook on domestic violence awareness.

BY BOB MEADE, MA
Marriage and Family Therapist

MFC 39311

He loves me, he hurts me, chaos reigns.
I love him, I hate him, fear remains.
Hope, disappointment, hope returns.
The cycle keeps spinning, deeper it burns.

Help! No more, no more. It's time.
Stop!

authorHOUSE®

AuthorHouse™
1663 Liberty Drive
Bloomington, IN 47403
www.authorhouse.com
Phone: 1-800-839-8640

First published by AuthorHouse 6/16/2009

ISBN: 978-1-4389-4017-5 (sc)
ISBN: 978-1-4389-4018-2 (hc)

Library of Congress Control Number: 2009904667

Printed in the United States of America
Bloomington, Indiana

This book is printed on acid-free paper.

Please Note

This document is neither a diagnostic nor a treatment manual. It is not to be considered a substitute for the DSM-IV, its derivatives, or any other resource used for the diagnosis of any mental disorder. It is not to be used as a stand-alone resource for the development of treatment plans, strategies, or interventions. Furthermore, it is not to be considered a totally authoritative resource on domestic violence.

It is intended as a sharing of information. Such information is based on personal readings, observations, consultations with other therapists, and various experiences, both mine, and those of past and present clients. These experiences are shared with their permission while, at the same time, maintaining their confidentiality.

Dedication

To

Marjaree Mason

I want to dedicate this book to the memory of Marjaree Mason. She was a vibrant, intelligent, and beautiful woman when, in 1978, she was cut down in the very beginnings of her promising life by the senseless acts of an abusive former boyfriend. Her death sparked a reaction that brought a community together to fight against the horrors of domestic violence wherever it is found, regardless of race, religion, financial status, or prestige. The work of the Marjaree Mason Center, which was opened soon after her death, continues today throughout the San Joaquin Valley of central California, with its headquarters in Fresno, California.

It is my hope that this work contributes, in some small way, towards those efforts. For more information on this agency contact:

Marjaree Mason Center
1600 M Street
Fresno, CA 93721

Or look it up on the Web at:
www.mmcenter.org

Table of Contents

Acknowledgments

There are so many people I want to thank who have had a part in helping me be where I am today and encouraged me in the writing of this book. There are, of course, too many to thank individually but there are those who truly stand out in helping me learn about domestic violence and being able to help those caught up in it.

First, major thanks to my wife **Marie**. She is a Licensed Clinical Social Worker (LCSW) herself and has been such a great, loving support in helping me put this material together. She has been so patient in waiting for me to get home late after sessions, or working with a distressed client, or teaching a class. She listens to me go over and over my thoughts out loud without committing me to an institution somewhere. She has empathized with me when things go wrong and celebrated with me when the successes come. Our long walks and "deep conversations" have been priceless for me. I wouldn't be here without her love and support, and appreciate her so much.

Also, a special thank you goes to my daughters, **Janet** and **Jennifer**. Jennifer has always encouraged me to "speak my mind" and to write this book. In answer to my fears of rejection, Janet has been quick to remind me that there are always those who will disagree with you as well as those who think you "walk on water." In part, I offer this book in response to their challenges to go ahead and say it as I see it. I also appreciate Janet's time and efforts in editing my very rough drafts and the input both girls have given as we've discussed aspects of the text. I am proud of both of them for reaching out to people in their lives, using the information in this book to help others.

I want to thank **Maureen Russell, LCSW** for guiding me through my internship as my supervisor and even more for the countless hours of teaching, sharing, and discussing domestic violence issues. To me she is one of the leading experts on the subject in the whole San Joaquin Valley of central California, and I appreciate her sharing her experiences and her insights. Her support has always been there, and a better friend I couldn't find.

A big thank you goes to **Dr. Barbara Hughes, Ph.D**. for her mentoring and great support. So many times we have sat and talked about mental health issues, from domestic violence to schizophrenia. She has challenged me in the best ways. She has always helped me to debrief, and give insights and instruction when I needed it, which has been often.

I also want to thank **Martha L. Cruz, MA**. She is one of the best bilingual domestic violence counselors in the greater Fresno area. We've spent many hours discussing materials found in this book. Her insights into personalities, cultural issues, and positive, constructive thought patterns have been great lessons for me. Also, her never-ending motivating support has been essential and so appreciated.

I further wish to thank one of my co-therapists, **Rondi Broesel, LCSW,** for her support as we've worked together in various ways. The many hours of clinical discussions and rehashing of various clinical issues have all helped me gain a better understanding of clients and ways to help them. Her encouragement and positive support have been awesome for me.

Meredith Fowler, RN, Licensed Marriage and Family Therapist (LMFT) also needs recognition and thanks. She has been a constant in my life for many years now, giving me great support and encouragement. Our clinical discussions and her sharing her thoughts have given me insights and validations probably far more than she knows.

I wouldn't be where I am today without the therapeutic help and support of **Jean Vavoulis, LCSW**. Over the ten years we worked together, she listened to me, challenged me, and encouraged me. Although she is now deceased, I can still hear her words and see her smile. Jean, I couldn't have done this without you.

I also have to thank **Kathy Rudy, MS** who has believed in me for many years and who has challenged me so many times to complete this work. She counsels and teaches students at Reedley College in Reedley, California, and has been such a wonderful support for me. She has provided me opportunities to teach at the school and to share my insights in efforts to help students in her classes over the years.

Another lady who has allowed me to share these insights with students is **Mary Shamshoian, MA, LMFT**. She is the Director of the On-sight Counseling Program at the Mennonite Biblical Seminary in Fresno, CA. I admire her efforts to train future counselors and educators about the particulars of domestic violence and I thank her so much for the opportunities she's given me.

Pam Lackey, MS has taught me so much about abusive personalities. Pam has been one of the best facilitators, in working with Batterer's Intervention programs, I've ever known. She continues to teach me so much regarding the actions of batterers and how they think. She is a true scholar who has shared her insights and who has kept me balanced in my viewpoints and thoughts.

I also wish to thank **Virginia Burgstrom, MA, LMFT** for her time spent discussing abuse issues and sharing with me how she approaches certain topics with clients. She has such a beautiful way of identifying with clients and helping them move step by step through difficult times.

I want to thank those working in the legal field as well. Fresno County Assistant District Attorney **Michelle Griggs** has been so patient in instructing me as to the ways of the law and the courts as well as encouraging me in the work I do with victims and perpetrators. She, and her associates who work in the domestic violence arena, faces such incredible challenges. I admire their efforts and applaud their work.

I also want to recognize and thank the attorneys who work as public defenders and defense attorneys, who provide the proper balance in our adversarial judicial system.

I cannot let the opportunity go by without thanking the counselors and staff at the **Marjaree Mason Center** in Fresno, California. This agency works tirelessly to provide shelter and counseling for victims of domestic violence and their families, as well as instruction for batterers. I have seen therapists, interns, trainees, and advocates work long, long hours to provide help, support, and education to people trying to escape abusive relationships. Staff members, from the executive director to the receptionist, from case managers to the accounting staff to the maintenance crews, all work together as a team to meet the goals of the agency. I believe Marjaree Mason herself would be very proud of this fine group of folks.

Most Important Thank You!

Perhaps the most important thank you is for the many clients, and others, I've worked with who have taken the courageous steps to get free from abuse and to learn about healthy relationships. Most people do not realize what an incredible thing it is to get out. I believe it is one of the most difficult and scary things a person can do. I admire these folks so much, and at times I think they've taught me more than I've ever been able to help them. To:

Tami, Aaren, Melissa, Alexandra, Mark, Jessica, Rhonda, Mari, Nancy, Rene, Pam, Rachel, Melody, Anne, Becky, Keli, Sharla, Sherry, Grace, Reina, Brenda, Katie, Kenny, Angelica, Barbara, Cindy, Patti, Heather, Betty, Francine, Cindi, Melanie, Jill, Balinda, Stacy, Bonnie, Mary, Tammy, Christina, Rena, Drew, Hafeez, Colleen, Rebeca, Sharon, Laura, Tracy, Carla, Michael, Patricia, Miriam, Belinda, James, Lydia, Maria ...

and so many others, past and present—I thank you for sharing your lives with me and hope that, in this work, I've done some small part to help others through sharing pieces of your courageous stories.

Before we start...

Before we start our look at the world of domestic violence, there are a couple of points I'd like to make.

First, watch out for *"one right answer"* syndrome. No, there isn't really such a syndrome or diagnosis. However, many of us suffer from this blinding mental process. We have been taught since childhood that there is "one right answer" to things. 2 + 2 = 4, correct? All through our schooling, test after test, we are told there is one right answer and are graded accordingly. Some parental guidelines are such that there is one right answer. Some religious folks live their lives according to the code of one right answer. Indeed, we can all find ourselves in a "box" mentally, and we don't even realize it. Granted, in some areas it seems there is only one right answer but even in those areas, so set in stone, I challenge you to dare to examine further. Question!

The reason I say this is that I have found life isn't this rigid. What appears to be "the one right answer" according to me isn't necessarily the same for you. We've all lived our lives and had our experiences and learned our lessons; we view things and events differently. In some areas of my life, I feel there is "one right answer" for me. That is my code, my beliefs, and my boundaries. It is … for me. However, I cannot dictate what is "the right answer" for you or for others. That is your decision and yours alone. I can reason with you, share with you, laugh with you, but when it comes to the moment to decide — it is your choice. It is not my place to say you are wrong either. I accept that it is your choice and what you think is right for you. If I disagree strongly enough, I can choose not to be around you, or choose to not have you as a friend or even a client. Those are my choices, for me.

So it is with my clients and with victims of domestic violence. I have clients who learn about domestic violence and see it happening in their lives and choose to stay in it. Is that wrong? Not according to them at the moment. In weighing the choices and consequences at that time, they feel it is the right thing for them to do. I most often disagree, but it is their choice, and as their therapist, I choose to walk with them and continue to support them. I do not see them as "crazy" or "mentally irregular." I see them, rather, as dedicated partners who are facing some of the most difficult, and oftentimes dangerous, decisions of their lives. They have dedicated their lives to making the relationship "work." They may have children involved and have tried so hard to make the "family" function as a family. They have "history" and a certain "chemistry" with their abusive partner. These are not easy things to walk away from, to let go, to give up on.

If they seriously consider leaving or ending the relationship and walking away, what are they walking to? The unknown is often more frightening than the abuse to which they've become accustomed. I've had several clients tell me, "If I'd known it would be this difficult to get my life going again, I might not have left at all."

Oftentimes, it is a month or two months later that I get a call or see a client who says, "Now! Now I have to get away!" It is their choice, and as a result, it strengthens them.

I share this to caution the reader not to judge so quickly those who decide to stay in an abusive relationship at that moment. Continue to support the "victim" even if from a distance. They will hopefully come around, as so many others have done, and see the timing, the opportunity, the choice, and take the steps to leave. If you have continued to support them, you will be there to help when the time is right.

I must add here that there have been those rare occurrences when a client has chosen to stay in the relationship and the abuser has actually taken the incredible steps to get better. Walking through a department store, I came face to face with a former client I hadn't seen in a long time. It had been several years and she was one of those clients I sometimes work with who simply stop coming to sessions; I don't hear from them and I never know what happened. I often find myself wondering about these dear souls.

"Bob!" she said. "How have you been?"

"Fine," I replied, "and you?"

"I'm great," was her reply. "I am the happiest I've ever been."

"Wow! That's wonderful. What all has happened since years ago?"

"Well, my husband went through the Batterer's Intervention program, and he really worked it. I did the counseling with you and then later we both went to church study groups. He really changed, and I'm so thrilled we stayed together! Now we have our own business together and I just can't explain how happy I am. Thank you so much for all the help you gave me way back then."

"You are most welcome," I replied and then she was gone. Sometimes, yes, sometimes it all works for both partners.

Second, always be aware of *"thinking outside the box,"* and keep in mind that there are different points of view on any given subject. How you see things may very well be very different from how I see them. I'll give you an example. My wife and I walk some mornings to get exercise. We go early, and during the winter months it is usually dark when we start out. As we went by a house one dark, early morning, I noticed the lights were on beside the garage. Each light had a metal plate covering it with holes in the plate, causing the light to throw shadowy images on the wall around the fixture. I didn't say anything to my wife as we walked by, but I wondered why a family would put up a fixture that made a monster face on their wall. Maybe it was to scare off would-be burglars at night. Or maybe it was a spiritual thing to keep evil away from the house. Who knows? Then, one day, as we walked by that same house, I couldn't help but point it out to her and asked, "Why would anyone want a monster's face on their wall?"

"What monster face?" she asked back.

"Right there," I said, pointing to the fixtures casting shadows on the garage wall.

"That's not a monster!" she smiled. "That's a butterfly!"

"A what???"

"A butterfly. Can't you see it?"

I stared at the shadows on the wall for at least a minute, and then suddenly, voila! I saw the butterfly. OK, so I'm not the fastest on the pickup sometimes.

"Oh wow," I stammered. "I've always seen it as a monster!"

Since that day, I always go by that house and tell myself, "Turn the monster into the butterfly!" Many times in my work, I've shared this story with clients facing some very difficult decisions. You can't change another person, but you can change how you think about them, how you see them, and decide whether you want to be around them or not.

So was I wrong to see the monster's face in the shadows? No, it was how I saw it, and still today I can see that face. But I also look at the shadows on that wall and see the beautiful butterfly my wife pointed out to me. We each have our ways of looking at the same set of facts, the same issues of life, and we see them differently. Be open to that. You may not be able to see it the same way, and that's OK. Work with it. Think outside the box.

Introduction

"I never knew! I've lived it for years and never knew!"

I've heard these words, or similar statements, many, many times working with domestic violence survivors. So many people, living as victims in abusive relationships, cannot see the forest for the trees. They live through it every day but cannot see it, and most feel one of two ways:

One, they are alone and no one can understand them or won't believe them.
Or
Two, all relationships must be this way and it is "normal."

The purpose of this assortment of materials is to dispel both of the above ideas.

First, there are those who understand what you are going through — many of whom have walked in your shoes.
And
Second, such abusive relationships are NOT normal.

It can be a very frightening thing to sit down with a therapist or counselor, a complete stranger, and start sharing your life story. I recognize this and put a very high value on the times I've spent with clients willing to share with me their everyday experiences, their successes and failures, dreams and disappointments, their "surface clutter" as well as their deepest, darkest secrets.

I have tried to learn from them and have sought to incorporate their experiences and life stories into this material. The best teachers of all are those who have lived the life, learned from it, and then are willing to share their stories. It is to these past, current, and future clients that I am forever grateful.

I have included in these pages assorted quotes, insights, and writings from survivors who have graciously shared parts of their stories. Each has done so with the hope he/she can somehow help those still caught in the abuse. They share also to help those who love and support such victims, to understand what they went through. I have also shared some quotations and object lessons, gathered across the hours of counseling, that seem to help some victims/survivors better understand where they've been, what they've been through, and empower them to move on to successful lives of their own, free from the abuse.

I also hope this material can help the families and loved ones of those caught in the web of abuse. It can be very confusing and, yes, frustrating and painful to try to reach out to someone you care so much about and have them reject your offers of help. What seems to be so obvious to you, she cannot seem to understand. They might even tell you, "I still love him!" after they've been beaten severely. There are reasons for this, and in this material I try to explain some of them as best I can with insights gained from working with clients. To those reaching out to loved ones in trouble, I say, "Be patient," and don't give up on them. Remain a supportive network and don't allow the abuser, or your own frustrations, to alienate you from your loved one.

I cannot stress this enough. One client who had been shot by her husband of many years came to me about our fourth session together and said, "I'm gonna tell you something, and then you can tell me to leave your office."

"What?" I asked.

"I still love him!" She almost flinched and ducked as she said it.

"Of course you do. There are parts of him that are loveable," was my reply.

She looked at me with eyes like saucers.

"But," I added quickly, "there's another part of him that's going to kill you if he gets the chance."

"I know and I struggle with that. But you are the only person who tells me it's OK that I still love part of him. All my relatives and friends are driving me insane with yelling at me that I must be mad to still love him. They taunt me with 'You must enjoy being shot.' I can't explain how I feel, but I just want to run somewhere, anywhere to get away — not from him, he's in jail — but from them!"

Despite the near abuse from her relatives, this client made great progress. She escaped the abusive world of her husband. After their divorce, she worked successfully in her own business, and last I heard, she was doing great.

Another client who was beaten severely by her partner found a place to stay with her sister and her family. As the days went by after the attack, she found herself at odds with the family as she tried to process with them that she was concerned for his well-being, as he was physically ill. Again, they questioned her sanity. This was one of the constant forms of abuse she suffered with her partner. She was always hearing "Are you really that crazy?" and "You're out of your mind." So one day when her sister said, "Are you really that crazy?" she packed up her stuff and went to the only other place she knew — yes, back with him. She explained it as, "At least I knew what to expect from him."

She eventually left him and was strong enough to make it on her own. He later died from his illness, and she was the one to take care of what little estate he had. She is now living her life and learning every day. She accepts life's challenges and maintains a great outlook on her world. However, her family is not much a part of that world. The pain caused by their rejection of her when she needed them most has left a very deep wound.

So continue to support your loved one. You may not understand where she's coming from. It might frustrate you and leave you speechless. What she needs is what she doesn't get from her partner. Acceptance and empathy, encouragement and even praise, are the lifelines that will help and support.

I recognize a certain dilemma in the use of pronouns in writing this text. It is generally considered that about 85 percent of abusers are male and that, far and away, the majority of victims are female. I have read some reports with statistics showing total abuse in a relationship is nearly 50/50 and that both partners abuse each other in equal amounts, although males tend to be more violent and cause more serious injury. For the sake of convenience only, in this text, I am using the pronoun "he" for the abuser and "she" for the victim. I fully recognize that there are male victims, and I have worked with many. I understand there is an equal amount of domestic abuse in the gay/lesbian/transgendered community as there is in heterosexual relationships. There are also those instances in which there is "mutual combat" and "co-combatants." To try to make statements that accommodate all the possibilities is simply too cumbersome. I hope the reader understands.

I do not intend this material as a program for the abuser, whether male or female. The work an abuser needs to do to improve himself requires a different approach, and I leave that for those who work in Batterer's Intervention programs or who do individual counseling with them.

I believe this book can be of help in understanding abuse from a victim's perspective but it does not even begin to touch on the issues the abuser faces within. Abusers can and do change for the better. It requires a lot of hard work that begins with the understanding that he/she is solely responsible for his/her abusive behavior. Each of us can have people "push our buttons" but when it comes time to speak and/or act, we make our own choice and are responsible for what we do. I have the highest regard and utmost respect for any abuser who reaches that point and truly begins to change. One key point here is that any change an abuser makes has to be for himself and not for the sake of the "couple" or the partner, or the children, or even the courts. The only way it "takes" is if the change is done for the self, and the self alone.

It is my intent to positively impact the lives of those who read these words, whether they are victims/survivors or the loved ones and friends of those who suffer in their abusive world. I hope to educate and support through this book. I believe it is only through such education and support that we can constructively work to eliminate domestic violence. I am not naïve enough to believe we can ever totally eliminate it, but the dream is there and very much alive. If these words can make a difference in one life, then that is one life closer to that dream. If it can help to stop the violence, whether physical, psychological, or verbal, in one person's world, then this work is a success. I thank you for reading it, sharing my thoughts, and supporting those struggling to understand, or just passing it on to someone else who might be helped by it.

Chapter 1

The Nature of Abuse

Domestic violence is a learned behavior. I don't look at abusers as animals or monsters foaming at the mouth with blood dripping from three-inch fangs. I don't think most of them are that mean and vicious to deliberately treat their victim/partner with such disdain. Note, I said "most." There are those who are just that mean and vicious and who do what they do with deliberate vengeance in mind. Most, however, I think, treat their partner this way because they've learned from childhood that this is how to treat an intimate "loved one." The abuser has learned to be abusive through watching and experiencing Mom and Dad, Grandma and Grandpa, or even an aunt and uncle. Somewhere, the abusive personality was formed by the experiences of the child in the home. In some cases, it's not the dad who is the abusive one, either. I've had several clients who struggle not only with their abusive boyfriend or husband but also with his mother, who shows herself to be just as abusive as the son. A common denominator in these situations is that his mom blames the victim for everything the son does wrong.

While most victims can describe their version of a "loving relationship" in terms of "loving," "caring," "nurturing," "sharing

1

intimacies," "trusting," and "respecting," an abusive person thinks in terms of "power" and "control." In my experience, the abuser has very little clue as to the nature of "nurturing" or "caring." Oh, he may say, "I love you," the same as his partner does. However, the meaning is different. The best way I know to put it is that, in the abuser's mind, "I love you," means, "You are an object I can control."

I deliberately use the word "object." The victim is not viewed as a person with thoughts and feelings that matter. The victim's dreams are inconsequential and, oftentimes, are felt by the abuser as a threat. Yes, a threat to his control. Her feelings are unimportant and are not understood and, again, are threatening. All that matters to the abusive personality is that he has control and that the victim does what he wants her to do when he wants her to do it, without questions. I know this is hard to comprehend. Imagine how hard it is to believe when you are in love with the abusive person. You simply don't want to believe this person you love feels this way or could be so cold-hearted. And yet, such behavior is repeated over and over again.

Later in this book we will look at the Dr. Jekyll and Mr. Hyde cycle of the abusive personality. Right now however, I want to point out that the abusive behavior is not a constant thing. If it was, the victim would have left long ago. What makes the whole thing so problematic is that the abuser, at times, is the nicest guy in the world. The man she fell in love with is "Prince Charming." He listens, smiles, laughs, and seems so understanding. Everybody loves Dr. Jekyll. Then suddenly he shifts, changes, explodes. Mr. Hyde appears and the victimization begins again. It is so confusing for the victim to have the man she loves appear for a while and then change into the monster who is so disrespectful.

There are those abusers who know exactly what they are doing when they are doing it. These are the worst and most dangerous. However, generally, I believe the abuser has very little insight into his emotions or motivations for what he does. One man, while under arrest for beating his wife, was asked why he did it. He responded, "I guess it was just time she got beat." In talking with facilitators of Batterer's Intervention programs, I've been told that, for many abusers, the only emotion they are really in touch with is anger. In today's society, it is common that men are raised to know anger and express it and be OK about it. Women are raised to know an assortment of emotions and to be in touch with them. This isn't the time or the place to carry on this debate about how we are raising our children, but it is definitely something to consider.

A metaphor I often use in my discussions with clients is my idea that we are all born with a workshop inside of us. As infants we walk into this workshop and find clipboards hanging on the walls. These clipboards all have titles on them of various aspects of our life. They have titles but nothing written underneath. It is for us to fill in the definitions and examples of each subject found on those clipboards, and I believe it takes a lifetime to identify them all. One of those clipboards has the title "Loving Relationship." Underneath that title we write what we experience as infants and children. I offer that we are hardwired, if you will, that what we see from our primary caregivers is what we write down on that clipboard. As infants, we don't know "right" from "wrong," "good" from "bad." We simply write down what we see and hear and feel. We take it at face value with no rationalizations. So, if what we see is fighting, we write that down. If it's arguing, hitting, yelling, throwing things, we write it down. There are also good times and laughter and playing. That gets written down too. So the clipboard script looks something like this:

LOVING RELATIONSHIP

Fighting	Getting gifts
Arguing	Laughing
Yelling	Joking around
Hitting	Fun
Throwing things	Hugs and kisses

According to my metaphor, this gets hardwired into our subconscious. Later, as adolescents, we start looking to find someone with whom to have a "loving relationship." By then we might have in our conscious mind the idea of the white-picket fence, the perfect "in-love" relationship. However, the hardwiring tells us different. So, when we find that boyfriend or girlfriend and we start having feelings for them, the clipboard script kicks in. Everything is going great, everyone is happy, but the subconscious says, "This isn't a loving relationship. Where's the fighting, where's the arguing?" So we act out and start fights. If the love interest of our life won't engage and fight back, then we feel they are "boring" and not a "good fit," and we dump them. We continue our search until we find someone who meets the criteria of our clipboard. Oftentimes, this is perplexing to our conscious mind, and we have to do a lot of rationalization to continue being "in love."

A couple of stories from clients' lives might cast a spotlight on this idea. I had a client come once because she was beaten. A gentleman had brought her and he was sitting in the waiting room during our session. As she described the details of her attack, I became concerned that this man was actually her abuser. I asked her about this because if so, I didn't want him in the waiting room.

"Oh no," she replied. "That's my husband."

A bit confused by this, I asked, "Then who is beating you?"

"My boyfriend," she answered.

Still trying to get my mind wrapped around her situation, I asked, "What's wrong with your husband?"

She replied, "There's nothing wrong with him. But he's boring."

Here is a situation in which this lady's clipboard said there needed to be fighting and arguing for it to be exciting "love." Her husband wouldn't fight with her, so she sought it from someone else. However, the husband was good for getting her help when things got rough. I only saw her that one time and have often wondered what happened to them.

Another lady I worked with for some time came to some amazing discoveries. She started with me as a result of an abusive relationship. She worked hard on learning about herself, learning boundaries, communication skills, and so forth. After several months, she met a man and started dating.

She would come in and tell me, "I've died and gone to heaven!"

"Yes?" I queried. "What does that mean?"

"He listens to me, he asks me what I think, he's great."

"Wonderful."

"Yeah," she said, "so why am I picking fights?"

She went on to describe how she'd "bit his head off" because he put his fork down on the wrong side of the plate. Yes, you read that right. We worked on the differences between the conscious mind, which says it's a match made in heaven, and the subconscious mind's "clipboard," which says there needs to be fighting for it to be a loving relationship.

Eventually, things got heated one day and she was yelling at him. He refused to engage and she yelled, "I know you don't love me because you won't fight with me!"

There was a moment of silence between them and then her boyfriend said, "Did you hear what you just said?"

"Yes," was her reply. "I need to call Bob."

In our session later that day, we discussed at length the conflict between her head and her "clipboard." She finally started "getting it" and began making changes.

I'm convinced the "clipboard" can be rewritten, but the conscious mind has to be on top of it on a daily basis. Step by step, moment by moment, we can catch ourselves and change that thinking. We can change the "clipboard" to read a definition that is what we feel today. I've seen many clients do it and go on to find healthy relationships.

I believe the difference for the abuser is that the clipboard reads "control" and "dominate" on that list under "Loving Relationship." It is how he survives. There is an incredible need for the so-called relationship. The abuser has to have that object in his life. This is one reason an abuser moves quickly to form a committed relationship. One client related that her abuser proposed to her after the first date and despite her saying "no," he showed up at her place the next day with all his stuff, ready to move in.

Often I have clients describe their abusers as "little boys," and indeed, this fits. The little boy inside is scared to death and has learned to survive through the use of powerful tactics meant to control and intimidate his intimate partner. Without such control, the little boy inside feels he's going to die. No, its not true, but the little boy feels that way, and as a result the fight to keep that control is fierce, a life-and-death fierceness.

I believe this is why the most dangerous time for a victim of abuse is when she is getting away. The statistics are incredibly high that victims who are fatally attacked or most seriously injured by their abuser are so attacked when they are trying to leave. There is no other time in the entire span of the relationship that the danger level is as high. Why? The abusive "little boy" is feeling the total loss of power over the victim, the object of his control. Thus he faces a life-and-death struggle inside and lashes out to take control back and save his life. This is also a reason it is so difficult for the abusive personality to change. Letting go of that control is so scary and frightening. Changing the script on that "clipboard" is one hellish job! It is one reason I have such high regard for any former abuser who has learned to live life in a healthy way.

Survivor's Corner

"It is what it is.

It's not what it was.
It's not what it could have been.

It just is what it is."

Becky

Chapter Two

The Tools of Abuse

Introduction to the Tools of Abuse Chart

In the following chapters I describe the "tools of abuse." By that I mean the various forms of abuse that a victim endures from the abuser. There are many different types of abuse, and I am highlighting just a few "tactics" most victims suffer through. These are all common denominators in the relationships my clients and others have lived with every day, 24/7.

The chart I've created highlights psychological, emotional, and verbal abuse tactics because every client I've ever had, to a one — and yes, I've asked each one — has said that the worst of the abuse is the psychological, emotional, and verbal and NOT the physical. This includes clients who have been shot, stabbed, raped, left for dead, or beaten severely. They all have told me, "The physical wounds heal, the bones set, the black-and-blue bruises go away, but what do I do with my mind and my heart?" On the outside they look "fine." Most people think they've recovered, but never could anything be further from the truth.

As one client told me, "My body will never be the same after the stabbing, true, but it has healed and I'm functioning. It's my mind that I can't seem to fix."

One of the problems with our society today is that we look for bruises. If a victim doesn't have bruises, then they must not truly be in a violent relationship. Indeed, the client who was in the worst shape of any I've seen, and who could barely function as a person, was never hit. Not once. But the mental and verbal abuse she suffered on a daily basis left her an empty shell, almost unable to break free. She did eventually but it was a long, hard road to recovery.

As I stated earlier, these are the day-in and day-out experiences that most others outside the relationship don't know about. The victim never tells anyone.

"It's too embarrassing to tell my friends."

"No one would believe me."

"If my friends knew what happens, they'd yell at me for not leaving."

These are some of the comments I hear when clients reveal their ordeals, and I ask if they ever told any of their relatives or friends. This is the "unknown world" of domestic violence and perhaps why I prefer to call it "domestic abuse," because there are no outward bruises from these forms of "violence." The victim is no less black and blue from the verbal and mental attacks but the bruises are all internal, and no one can see them.

As you look at the chart, I have listed some of the ways victims experience these psychological, emotional, and verbal attacks in the hopes of enlightening others as to their plight. One client called it "domestic terrorism," and from that you can see the impact and significance of what victims go through. I so appreciate clients sharing these events with me, and I applaud their courage in doing so.

THE TOOLS OF ABUSE

Psychological, Emotional, Verbal

PSYCHOLOGICAL	EMOTIONAL	VERBAL
Body language Clenched fists Body stance Look in the eye Facial expressions	**Put downs** You're stupid You're fat You can't do anything Nobody wants you	**Name calling** Think of the ugliest names you know and fill them in here.
"Weapons" Use of objects and weapons meant to scare victim into compliance	**Abuse or Kill Pets** Uses emotional attach- ment to animals to show victim what to expect if they disobey.	**Verbal threats** Threatens to kill, take away the children, hurt in some way, hurt victim's family
Reality shifts Getting the victim to doubt her/his sense of reality and imposing their own.	**Crazy - Making** Crazy - making mind games played on victim's emotions and thoughts	**"Crazy" talk** "Everyone knows you're crazy!" "Who's going to believe you?"
Denying Access Isolates victim by stifling access to friends, family, church, or other forms of support	**Emotional Rifts** Creates emotional rifts between victim and her friends and family.	**Accusations** Verbal attacks and accusations of cheating, scheming, lying, etc.
"Relationship" Manipulation Uses victim's concept of "relationship" against her/him	**Plays On Emotions** Knows victim's emotional "buttons" and turns them to use as emotional weapons	**"Sounds good"** Abuser appears genuinely interested but then uses victim's words against her/him

Eventual Outcomes

Learned Helplessness Creates mental state in which victim believes she/he is helpless to change the situation and cannot escape.	**Emotional Numbness** Victim no longer feels the emotional reactions to the abuse and accepts it as "the way life is".	**Verbal Acceptance** Victim "accepts", and verbally agrees, that the problems are all her/his fault.

Domestic Violence Awareness 2005

Chapter Three

Abuse by Familiarity

The following tactics develop as the relationship progresses and various forms of intimacy grow. The abuser learns the victim's emotional and verbal vulnerabilities, while the victim becomes familiar with the abuser's non-verbal cues.

Body Language

Relationships experience several forms of intimacy. These include mental, emotional, spiritual, and physical. The physical side of the relationship is so important. This isn't based on physical beauty or ugliness, size or shape, or even color. It's the closeness we have with each other in the form of physical bonding that takes place. In a healthy relationship, there is a sense of closeness, security, acceptance, and respect for each other's body and physical presence. Indeed, the physical intimacies are perhaps the most vulnerable we can be with a partner. We learn to recognize body movements and body language. So much is said without saying a word. We learn to recognize the slightest nuances in the body language. A look, an action, a gesture is all it takes, and we know what they're thinking. These are critical elements in any relationship.

In the world of the abuse victim, the physical side of the relationship can be exciting one moment and terrifying the next. Many times, I've had clients describe incredible sexual chemistry with their abusive partner and then tell me about some of the body language they've learned to read that tells them an attack is imminent. This dual relationship creates psychological havoc for the victim.

Certain body language actions I've heard described include clenching fists, tightening shoulders, grinding teeth, certain body stances, and changes in facial expressions. One of the most common elements, and perhaps the most frightening, is the change in the face and the eyes of the abuser as he is about to attack, or is attacking. Most every client has told me about how his eyes would change. Some describe them as becoming "lifeless"; others talk about how big they get, or how small they get. The descriptions may differ but the impact is the same. "Frightening" is putting it mildly. For most victims, it is terrifying to see because they know what's coming. However, I've learned that just because the eyes change, or the face changes, doesn't mean they will attack; at least, not yet.

One client described the scene in the courtroom after the judge awarded her custody of her child and child support from her ex-husband. Her ex looked around his attorney and caught her eye. His face was brutally hard, his eyes were "dead," and his shoulders and chest were taut like he was going to break the table. Then his attorney turned to speak to him and in a moment he was smiling, shaking hands. He looked totally relaxed. No one else noticed the instantaneous transformation. However, she got the message. In that look of just a few seconds, she knew there would be hell to pay for the court's decision.

I remember reading that Alfred Hitchcock said it wasn't the bang that scares us but rather the anticipation of the bang. This is the psychological abuse the victim goes through daily. The anticipation of the violence is generally worse than the violence itself. I remember a lady telling me that she and her partner went out with another couple one night. Something was said or done, but she couldn't recall what it was. However, looking across at him, she found him staring at her with "that look," as she called it. It didn't matter what she did or said after that. It didn't matter that she didn't have a clue what she had supposedly done wrong. She only knew she was in for it when they got home. For the rest of the time with the other couple, she was totally preoccupied with the dreaded expectations. The other couple had no idea any of this was going on as far as the lady could tell.

Another act of "body language," if you will, occurred to a lady who was beaten by her husband so badly that she needed medical attention. He drove her to the ER at the nearby hospital. As she was being examined, the doctor asked how she was hurt. Her husband was standing right there next to her. She hesitated to come up with a story for the doctor's questions. The husband spoke up and provided the details of how she fell down and hit her head on the end table. Sensing something wasn't right, the doctor asked the husband to step outside the room while the doctor continued the examination. The husband did so and the doctor closed the door. As the doctor began asking again about the injuries, the lady could hear her husband just outside the door, swinging his keychain back and forth with a distinctive clicking noise. He was listening through the door, and she knew he could hear every word. So she told the doctor exactly what the husband had said earlier. The lady indicated that although those injuries healed and the bruises were long since gone, the sound of that keychain still haunted her in nightmares at least twice a week. Even now, hearing a sound similar to it startles her and she jumps every time. Mind you, she left the man about three years ago, and still she is bothered by it.

Often clients describe the aftermath of attacks in generalities. They can't remember the exact bruises or broken objects in the house after an incident. They can describe in great detail, though, the facial expressions and body language of the abuser before, during, and after an attack. They close their eyes and see him standing there. One client described it as "haunting" and "never-ending." This has a devastating impact on the victim psychologically and is very difficult to overcome.

Put-Downs

Another aspect of this non-physical physical tactic is the verbal assault that leaves her emotionally drained and hurting. There is verbal name-calling, but this is a little different. The victim constantly hears belittling comments about her physical appearance or her choices in clothes or some other physical aspect of who she is. Most clients are bruised and battered by this regularly. I've long since lost count of the number of clients who are told by their abuser how ugly they are or how fat they are.

One client laughed as she told me she didn't understand the contradictions in her husband's remarks. He was always telling her how ugly she was and that "no one would ever want to be with you." In the next few minutes, he would tell her that he knew she was sleeping around on him.

"Well, which is it?" she would ask him. "Am I so ugly no one wants to be with me, or am I so desirable that everyone wants to be with me?" She said she never got a straight answer but it generally upset him for her to ask.

Clients experience a roller coaster of emotions when dealing with their partner. One client told me that she and her husband were going to go out for an evening on the town. She was so thrilled because he didn't do this very often. She got ready and stood in front of the full-length mirror upstairs in their bedroom. She felt perfect. Her hair, her make-up, her dress and shoes, everything was perfect. She told me she felt so good, she was spinning around in front of the mirror to watch how beautiful her dress looked. She was on an emotional high.

She went downstairs. She approached her husband with a big smile on her face, anticipating his approval and a certain "oh wow" look in his eyes. Instead, he looked her up and down and said, "You're gonna wear that?" She was crushed. He then told her what to wear and ordered her upstairs to change. As she stood in front of the mirror again, she found herself saying, "Maybe I didn't look as good as I thought." In working with her, I asked her what changed between the first look in the mirror and the second. The dress was the same, the hair was the same, and the make-up was the same. The only thing different was that now she was feeling the emotional effects of what he said and how he had put her down. Based on that, and that alone, she was putting herself down and hoping she could please him by wearing what he told her to wear. She had been so happy earlier and felt so sexy. The rest of the evening she was just trying to keep him happy.

Another client experienced an ordeal that left her shaking her head in total confusion, and I don't believe she'd ever told anyone until relating it to me in a session. She and her husband had three children, all under the age of six. He worked full time and she stayed home with the kids. As a stay-at-home mom with three small children, she wasn't one to get dressed up. She was usually in sweats or jeans, as she had to be with the children all day.

One night, he came home from work and proceeded to verbally assault her on the fact she was always in grubby clothes. She tried to explain that she was with the children but it didn't matter to him. He yelled at her that other men's wives dressed up for them but she never did for him. This went on most of the night. She was determined not to let her husband down again.

So the next evening she was ready. She fixed her hair, she put on a dress and nylons, and did her make-up. She was ready, and when he came home and opened the door, she was there with open arms.

"Hi honey," she said.

He looked at her for a moment and then, rather than smiling and commenting on how nice she looked, he responded with, "You b____, I finally caught you! Who have you been with? Where have you been? What's his name?"

Several expletives were intermixed in the questioning. Despite her efforts to explain that the night before he had told her how mad he was that she never dressed up and she wanted to please him, he wasn't listening. He yelled at her all night with threats and comments about how ugly she looked and how stupid she was to wear that dress. He accused her of all manner of things. Eventually, it got down to his checking her underwear. I can't imagine how demeaning and embarrassing it must have been for her.

I asked her what she did the next night since she wasn't going to ever "get it right." She answered that since she was going to get yelled at, she might as well be comfortable during the yelling. So, she wore her sweats. By the way, the next night he came home with a smile on his face and went about the night joking and laughing with her. She was relieved but on eggshells. When would he blow up again and for what?

The effect of this emotional abuse is to leave the victim broken, confused, and feeling very low inside. Her self-esteem is zero and she figures she can never make it on her own and that she has no future except with him. She becomes dependent on him and clings to the slightest hint of a compliment or simply that he is almost happy with her. In some of the worse scenarios I've heard, the abuser tells the victim she did a good job only to say she could have done better or that another woman he used to know did it better. She begins to believe she can never get it right and that it's all her fault. The abuser will drive home the point that they could be really happy together if she would just stop messing up. She holds dearly to that dream of them being happy and so blames herself for everything that seems to prevent that happiness.

Name-Calling

Verbal abuse in this area usually includes sexually degrading name-calling. Often the abuser gets to know what the victim hates the most and will use those words or phrases every time. I could list some of the words here but you know what they are. As I said in the chart, imagine the ugliest words you know and fill them in. The constant use of these derogatory words and phrases tends to break down the victim, and she begins to see herself as less than other people. Her mental body image becomes twisted and illogical. She's heard the statements so many times, she's started believing it herself. She really is what he calls her.

The words used are not always vulgar. Sometimes, it's calling her fat or sloppy or lazy. I remember a lady who did all the work around the house but her abusive partner called her lazy every day. She never could get it right or work hard enough to please him. She turned this on herself to believe that she simply couldn't get enough done in a day and that it was all her fault things were difficult around the house. She said it was amazing that such a wonderful man would stay with her despite her shortcomings. You can see how she had totally bought into his abuse.

Victims carry these things in their minds every day. The name-calling, the emotional roller coaster, the body language all play into their view of the physical world. Oftentimes, you can tell them something and they don't believe you. A client came to my office one day. She was stunningly beautiful. She referred to herself, however, as "the ugly duckling." Why? Her boyfriend called her that nearly every day. He was always telling her she had the potential to be the beautiful swan but she was just an "ugly duckling." No matter what she tried to do to improve, it never worked as far as she was concerned. She worked out, she ate right, and she dressed impeccably. Still, she wasn't good enough for him. So did she leave him? No, she stayed and kept trying to make him happy. I don't know that she ever told anyone else about being "the ugly duckling." I do know that she thinks those thoughts, and hears those words in her mind and heart, every day and night.

With these thoughts in mind, you can see why it would be so difficult for a victim to leave an abusive relationship. Mentally and emotionally, they are hardly prepared for such a step into a world they feel views them as ugly, fat, a failure, a lost cause, stupid, a waste of time … and it's all their fault. Some would rather stay and accept the abuse they are familiar with than risk the rejection and failure they feel awaits them in the outside world.

Survivor's Corner

"He can't be calm ...
Unless he's in a state of chaos."

Rebecca

Chapter Four

Threats of Violence

In this chapter, I want to discuss the threats of violence the victim encounters all the time in the course of the relationship. These are merely threats and not actual violence to her person. However, to the victim, the threat has more impact mentally and emotionally than the actual act. I've actually had clients tell me they have deliberately invoked his wrath and "forced" him to attack her physically just to get him to stop threatening to attack.

Weapons

In the chart, I describe the use of weapons. By weapons I don't just mean guns and knives and swords. Oftentimes, these weapons are baseball bats or sticks or any other object that is meant to hurt. However, in dealing with the psychological abuse, the weapons are not used to physically harm but rather to mentally intimidate. In using them this way, the abuser scares the victim into compliance and submission. This doesn't have to be done in the heat of an argument. I've known of several instances when everything was fine and the abuser used a weapon to simply make a point.

One such incident occurred while a lady was playing with her children on the floor in the dining room of her home. Her abusive partner arrived home with a new butcher block and a set of knives to put in it. As he went through the knives, he discovered there was an extra one in the set. It was large and heavy. As the lady sat on the floor with the children, he came and knelt down, showing her the knife. He talked about how it was an extra and no one would know it was missing. If he were to kill someone with it, he told her, he could just throw it away and no one would know it ever existed. There wasn't even an empty slot for it in the block. He told her to look at how thick the blade was and how shiny. He ran the blade across her chest and up under her throat, all the while he was describing that because it was so thick and strong, it wouldn't break if it went through bone and flesh. He forced her to look at it as he described the damage it would do to someone if he were to use it that way. Now, he never said he was going to kill her with it. He simply described how easy it would be to kill someone, anyone, and get away with it. He then stood up, put the knives away, and went on about his business. About an hour later, the lady's eleven-year-old daughter turned to her and asked if Daddy was going to kill her with that knife. The lady told her that Daddy was just playing around. But the daughter knew better.

"If he kills you with that knife, I'll tell the cops that it was an extra and that he threw it away," she told her mom.

This lady never told anyone about that incident until she related it to me. Her family has no idea, and her friends would be totally shocked. But she has carried that memory in her mind for over a year. Even though she's gotten away from him, she still fears what he will do with that knife.

In other instances, I've heard clients tell of their abusers using objects to intimidate while the couple argued. One gentleman would always pick up a bat and work his hands around the handle the whole time they fought.

"He's never swung it at me," his partner explained, "but he works that handle like crazy and I'm so afraid that one day, one day ..."

Another abuser would pick up a baseball and rub it and toss it from hand to hand as they discussed things. She had seen him throw that ball against the wall and into a bookcase before and constantly feared that his next target would be her head.

Again, the intimidation factor is what is so devastating in these situations. One client described how every night when they went to bed, he would wait for her and make sure she watched as he fluffed his pillow. Under his pillow he kept a .32 caliber handgun. He would turn the gun so that the barrel pointed at her pillow and then place his fluffed pillow back on top of it. He never once picked it up and pointed it at her, but every night she knew it was there. Every night she laid her head down on her pillow, wondering if this was going to be the night. Did she ever tell her neighbors about it? No. Did she ever tell her best friend about it? No. Did she ever tell her mother about it? No. But she carries the memory still and sees that gun like it was just last night, although she's been gone from him for many years.

Abuse or Kill Pets

Those of us who love pets know we can form a very close emotional bond with the animal(s). They become like a member of the family. For some who have no children or other close relatives, the pet is the closest of friends and a companion for life.

In the victim's world, the abuser may torture, or even kill these pets to make a point. Victims realize that "if he will abuse the family pet, then he will certainly do the same to me." Clients have related being told by their abuser that if they don't do what he tells them to do, then the dog will pay for it, or she'll never see her favorite cat again. Indeed, I've had several clients who have left the house or the relationship and later returned to get their dog or cat or fish, only to find them gone or dead. One lady had a large fifty-five-gallon fish tank with her beautiful tropical fish she'd had for years. They were her pride and joy. When she returned to the house to get the tank and the fish, she found he had poured bleach into the water and killed everything inside. She dared to leave him, and she paid for it.

The abuser has no emotional connection to the pet. It turns out to be nothing more than an object he can use to hurt her, to get her attention, or just to show her who's boss.

I have heard of one situation in which the abuser would attack the victim and her dog would come and stand beside her. She warned him that one day he would attack and the dog would attack back. His reply was usually that he would take care of the dog without a problem. One day he attacked her and her son stepped in to defend her. The stepfather turned on the boy and the dog turned on him. This full adult Rottweiller grabbed his arm, bit to the bone, and wouldn't let go. The dog proceeded to maul the man until the family finally got it off of him. The lady described later that there was blood everywhere, and all of it was her abuser's. Eventually, the police arrived and he was taken to a hospital. He never returned to bother the lady, or her children, again. The dog, however, was changed forever. He was no longer able to relax with the family but rather would snap at them. Shortly after this attack, he had to be put down. He gave his life for the safety of his owner and her family.

Verbal Threats

These can be verbal threats to kill. Such threats are usually directed at the victim, but oftentimes they are more effective if they are told to the victim but directed at someone else. Many clients have heard the abuser threaten to kill them several times. The worst threats are made against her parents, or her siblings, or her children, or even against the abuser himself.

I've had clients tell me they stayed with him because he said that if she left, he would kill her parents or kill all her children or even kill himself.

One such client had on her cell phone voice mail a recording of him threatening to kill all of her children and cut them up and leave the pieces all around her home if she didn't let him come back. It can get graphic and is intended to intimidate, and it works!

Another client had a best girlfriend her abuser couldn't stand to have around. She and her friend had been buddies ever since grade school. One day, in a jealous rage, he told her that if she didn't stop seeing this girl then he would "take her out," and no one would ever see her again. He added that he had killed someone before and no one had ever found that body, so he'd put the friend's body there too. She called the friend and said she couldn't see her anymore. Eventually, after she'd left him and moved on, she reconnected with her friend.

I mentioned that the abuser could threaten to kill himself. This is actually quite common. I've had several clients tell me about incidents in which their partner grabbed a knife and put it to his own throat. One did so in front of his wife and two small children. You can imagine the chaos in that house as Dad stands in front of Mom and the kids and puts the knife to his own throat and tells her, "If you don't do what I tell you to do, then I'm gonna kill myself right here and now!"

The children were screaming, "Daddy, don't!"

The wife was screaming. This ordeal went on for almost an hour, with him eventually locking himself in the bathroom. She and her children were at the door, calling to him and begging him to stop. He came out, put the knife down, and left the house. He came back a short time later, smiling, and wanting to have sex. She agreed even though she was confused and hardly "in the mood." She was so relieved to have him back and happy.

Another client told me that her partner had threatened to kill himself so many times she no longer took him seriously. One night they got into a fight, and he went into the bedroom and got his gun. With his loaded gun in hand, he walked into the living room, cocked the hammer back, and said he would take care of all her problems for her by taking himself out.

She replied, "Stop! Stop! Get some plastic and put it down on the floor. I'm gonna have to clean up the mess, so make it easier for me."

With that said, she walked down the hall into the bedroom and closed the door. He put the gun down and followed her, saying he was sorry.

In relating these stories, I must add there are those situations in which abusers have indeed taken their own lives because the victim has left them. I believe such times are rare, but they do happen. It is important to note that for some abusive personalities, the loss of the object of their control leaves them alone and lost. It is not a state to be taken lightly.

There are other types of verbal threats the abuser uses to play mind-control over the victim. A classic one is that he will take the children with him if she leaves him. This is very effective against the victim when it is combined with other elements of abuse over time. If he has convinced her that no one will believe her, that she is crazy, and if he has effectively isolated her so she has little to no support, then telling her he will get the kids if she leaves is very believable to her. So she stays to protect the children. I cannot count the number of clients I've had who have stayed in the relationship to protect their children from the abuser.

This usually works until she sees the children begin to act exactly as the abuser does. I've known of two-year-olds calling their mom "b____" and worse. I had a client whose six-year-old son walked up to her one day, kicked her in the leg, and demanded, "Make me breakfast, b____!"

Needless to say, she was totally shocked, and yet that is what he had heard his father say to her many, many times over his few years of life.

This brings a whole new level of verbal abuse and verbal threats into her life. She finds little to no support from her partner to discipline the children. Usually what I hear is the partner blaming her and saying the child wouldn't act that way if she were more obedient to him, or if she just did what she was supposed to do.

Long after the physical abuse has stopped and the victim has gotten away, these statements and actions play over and over again in the client's mind. Clients can quote the abuser's threats and comments word for word years after they've left or he's gone to prison. They hear the sounds, notice similar actions in their everyday lives, or hear the words, and mentally, emotionally, they go back in time and re-experience the drama.

Chapter Five

Reality Shifts

In this chapter, I want to discuss one of the most difficult areas of psychological abuse the victim has to overcome. It is as close to brainwashing as I think one can come and has such a long-lasting effect on the victim's reasoning, thought processes, and emotional stability.

Reality Shifts

One day, a client of mine was going to go visit some friends. As she got to the door, her husband met her there and slammed the door shut. He questioned where she was going, and her reply was that she was going to go visit some friends, as she'd mentioned to him before. He informed her, as he grabbed her arm and pushed her down in a chair, that she wasn't going anywhere. She told me that they argued for almost half an hour about why she couldn't go and her reasons for wanting to go visiting.

Eventually, according to the client, he sat back in his chair, threw up his hands, and said, "Fine, fine, go visit your friends."

She hesitated a moment, smiled, and got her purse and headed for the door. He again met her at the door, slammed it shut, and asked her where she was going. She again replied that she was going to go visit her friends. He looked at her with astonishment and said, "You've got to be kidding! After all we've talked about, you would still disobey me and go?"

"No," she said. "You just said it was OK to go."

"I said what?" he asked.

"You just threw up your hands and said fine, go visit your friends." She motioned with her hands, mimicking his movements.

"Have you really lost your mind that bad?" was his comeback. "Why would I do that? After all we discussed and I told you no. Now you say I told you OK?"

"But you did!" she stammered.

"Oh my God, you really are crazy!" he replied. "You're not going anywhere. It's not safe for you to leave home. Sit back down in that chair, get your head together, and get back to doing what you need to do around this house."

She sat back down in the chair and figured she must have heard him wrong. Maybe she misunderstood his motions. Maybe she really was losing her mind like he said.

Scenes similar to this play out in abusive households every day. One day the victim does something "wrong" and the abuser tells her how bad she is and what he expects of her. He'll go to great lengths telling her she is so dumb and how it should be done. The next day, she does exactly what he told her to do and she is yelled at and ridiculed for doing it wrong again. She knows she understood what he said. She knows she did it just the way he told her. Now, however, she's second-guessing herself and figures she really is crazy or she needs to listen better or she is such a failure she'll never get it right.

The fact is, she heard him right. She did it exactly the way he said he wanted it done. She understood him just fine. However, he cannot let her be right. He has to have drama, and one of the best ways to do it is to create these paradoxical situations.

He says one thing and then later says he never said that and accuses her of twisting his words. He controls her every step but accuses her of controlling him. He's the one who hurts her but is always saying how much he loves her and can't understand why she's always hurting him. He's the one who has several other women around but he is always accusing her of cheating on him.

There is a purpose in all this. If he can get her to doubt her sense of reality, then he has her. He will dictate to her what "reality" is, and it will be according to him. It will change from day to day or even hour to hour. She is constantly off-guard and off-balance. He then controls her and her environment.

Crazy-Making

This is what I call "crazy-making" behavior. These are mind games that work to break down the victim mentally and emotionally. The victim loses all sense of personal validation. She doubts herself, and in her mind she begins to rationalize that he must be right. She's always apologizing for her mistakes. I had a client who would always say she was sorry during the first few sessions. One day, I stopped her and asked her why she was sorry.

"For being such a problem for you," she said.

"You are no problem for me," was my reply. "You just be you and tell me what you are feeling."

"I don't know what I'm feeling. I just know I'm a problem for everybody and I'm grateful you are putting up with me."

At the time of those statements, her husband had been dead for about a year. He died after a long illness, during which she had nursed him along and helped him. Hospice folks told her what a good job she was doing but he always insulted her and said she was a failure and that his illness was all her fault. She believed him and felt if she'd only been a better person, then he might still be alive. Despite doctor's findings and reports, she still felt she failed him. She said he always told her how crazy she was and that she couldn't do anything without messing it up. Now she guessed he was right.

It took a long time and a lot of work for her to begin to recognize her own self-worth again. Every step of the way, she figured there was no use doing anything because she'd just mess it up anyway. She was crazy and she might as well just accept it. She appreciated my help but I needed to know there was no hope for her. Still, she came every week.

She came in one day and told me she'd been thinking about all we had gone over. Someone had asked her a question earlier in the week and she'd answered it. The person came back later and thanked her and told her she was right and that it had really helped to get that information from her. Suddenly it hit her—she was right! Her answer was right! The mental fog started to lift.

"I'm not as dumb as I was told I was!" she exclaimed. "I know what's real and what isn't!" I believe it was at this point she began to heal emotionally. She began to trust herself again, ever so slightly. Her attitude began to change for the better. It was as if a dim light bulb suddenly went on somewhere in the recesses of her heart and she began to see. From that moment on, she began to change back to the lady she had been before her husband warped her reality with his crazy-making actions and statements.

This mind twisting and reality shifting has a long-lasting effect on the mental and emotional state of the victim. As I said with the lady before, it was a long hard journey filled with lots of doubts, second-guessing, and tears.

Crazy Talk

A constant during this crazy-making behavior is the crazy talk. Victims are always being told they are nuts. I've known several situations in which the abuser has gone on the Internet and found a diagnosis for bipolar disorder or borderline disorder or even schizophrenia; he then convinces the victim that the diagnosis fits her. I've long since lost count of the number of clients who have come into my office and told me in the first session that they were bipolar. When I ask what doctor or therapist diagnosed them, they say they haven't seen a doctor or another therapist. Their husband or boyfriend found the "diagnosis" and it "fit her". So that explained why they needed so much help.

In this particular situation, I want to address an observation of mine in working with clients over the years. One of the worst situations is when the victim's abusive partner is a doctor. Such a professional has the power to tell other doctors what their partner's "symptoms" are, and they can convince the psychiatrist or therapist to arrive at that diagnosis. Thus, she gets labeled as whatever he wants.

I had a client once who came in with her head down, slumped shoulders, and overall depressed look. She described her actions and interactions with her husband, who was a well-known medical doctor in the town where they lived. From what she told me, it was clear that he was very abusive to her mentally and verbally. Name-calling was an everyday event, and he knew just the right words to say to debase her. He was physically abusive in that he pushed her and pulled her hair, but never anything that would leave a mark or a bruise. There were certain physical acts he would make her do that weren't sexual but very demeaning. She never did tell me all of them but what she did tell me was deplorable.

She said that he had told her she was bipolar and proceeded to show her pages of information from the Internet to "prove" to her he was right. He accused her of doing things that she didn't remember ever doing. He told her she said things she didn't remember saying. She caught him once taking family pictures off the dresser in the bedroom and putting them in his drawers. She didn't say anything at the time, and he didn't know she'd seen him. A day later, she walked into the bedroom to find him standing there with his hands on his hips.

"Did you and your boyfriend have fun?" he asked.

"What boyfriend?" she questioned. "I have no boyfriend, you know that."

"Oh sure you do. Every time he comes over you put all the family pictures away. This time you forgot to put them back!" he exclaimed.

"No," she said. "I saw you put those pictures in your drawer yesterday." She walked over, opened the drawer, and pulled them out.

"I didn't know those were there," was his reply. "The only way you knew where to find them is because you put them there before your friend came over."

She told me she stared at him for a few seconds and left the room totally confused. This is a form of verbal "crazy-making." She never knew what to expect from him. However, at this point she was able to confirm what she'd seen him do and began planning on getting out of the relationship.

He had insisted they go to couple's counseling. During the first session, he told the therapist how much he loved his wife and cared for her. He talked about how hard he was trying to help her get through her hard times. The more he talked, the more upset she got. When it was her time to talk, she expressed her stress and unhappiness. She explained that he was abusive and driving her crazy. He interrupted to tell the therapist that from his position as a doctor, he knew she was bipolar and that explained her reactions and accusations. When the therapist nodded in agreement, the wife lost it. She cried as she told the therapist, "You're believing him and turning on me!"

Her husband spoke again, saying, "You see what I have to deal with all the time."

The therapist agreed she needed help and referred them to a psychiatrist. Of course, he knew a psychiatrist who would see them right away. My client told me that as they left the appointment, he began verbally berating her.

As she related it to me, he said, "How could you embarrass me like that in front of a professional therapist? You are so unappreciative of the help I'm getting for you. You don't know anything. You're stupid. You're lucky to have me when there are so many other women in town who would love to have me. But, no, I have to be with a sick dummy like you!"

The psychiatrist they went to was a friend of his. He described to the doctor all the symptoms he'd "seen" in her, and within a few minutes the diagnosis was written up. She was bipolar. The psychiatrist prescribed medication for her but her husband never allowed her to fill it. So I asked if she was taking anything for being bipolar, and she said, "No." Over the next several sessions, she related other events she'd gone through. She explained the impact on her two children as she saw it. We went over various aspects of domestic abuse. Each session she sat with her hands in her lap, her head down, and barely making eye contact.

After about five or six sessions, I said as we were closing, "You know, you're not crazy."

"What?" she asked. "What did you just say?"

"I said you're not crazy and as far as I can tell, you are not bipolar."

"How can that be? I've been told so many times that I am."

"I don't see any symptoms, and you're not taking any medication for it. If you truly were bipolar, then there should be signs of it in your attitude and actions, especially given what you're going through at home. I simply don't see any. So I don't think you are bipolar, and you're definitely not crazy."

"Wow!!" she exclaimed. "For once, someone thinks I'm sane!!" and with that she walked out the door.

The next week, she came to session and I hardly recognized her. Her hair was done, her head was up, and her eyes were virtually gleaming.

"My goodness," I said, "what a change in you."

"I know," she replied, "ever since you told me I'm not crazy I've felt so much better. I'm helping out at my son's school again and I'm even going to join a support group for mothers with difficult children!"

Her life had taken off. Her husband was very upset with her and was being extremely manipulative at home. He was telling her that she was crazier than ever and he might have to shut down his practice to take care of her. This was all his verbal crazy talk and mental manipulations used in an effort to shut her down. None of it was effective, as far as I know. We worked together for about another month or two. She separated from him and was living in her own place and doing very well, last I heard.

One of the effects of "crazy talk" is that it dovetails with other aspects of the tools of abuse. I will point this out later when we talk about the eventual outcomes of all this abuse on the client.

Survivor's Corner

"Even though I made a mistake,
it doesn't mean I am a mistake!"

Tami

Chapter Six

Isolation Tactics

One of the abuser's tactics in controlling his victim/partner is isolating her away from any and all support. This is done in a variety of ways and is very common in abusive relationships, so much so that it goes almost without asking when I'm initially talking with a client. I simply ask, "How is he isolating you?" and they tell me. In this chapter, I want to explain some of these tactics and give a couple of examples.

Denying Access

The process I usually hear about is that first the abuser works to get rid of the partner's friends. These folks might have been friends for years but he will create a rift between them and the partner. How does he do this? Many times it's not direct but rather by innuendo. He might make comments that her friends don't like him and he doesn't want to be around them. He then manipulates her time so she can't spend time away from him and be with her friends. If he picks up that she intends to get together with them, he'll be "sick" or there will be car trouble so she can't go or any of other assorted reasons. The bottom line is she doesn't get together with her friends. If this happens often enough and long enough, she loses contact with them.

I've known clients whose abusers tell them they can go see their friends but as soon as they leave to go visit, he starts "blowing up" their phone with calls every five minutes or more. These calls are asking when she's going to come home and/or questions about who she's really with and whether men are there. If she answers the call, she has to explain what she's doing. If she doesn't answer the phone, there will be hell to pay later when she gets home or sees him again. I had a client who refused to answer her phone one night when she was out with her girlfriends. He literally called her fifty-eight times in thirty minutes in the form of phone calls and voicemails and text messages. This is something I've seen many female abusers do to their male victims. Just change the pronouns.

Other situations include partners being told to go have a good time but be back by a certain time. If she's not back at or before that time, they know they're in for it, whether verbally or physically or both. One lady was to be home at 4 p.m. At 3:50 p.m., she called from her girlfriend's house and told him she was on her way home. As she walked up the sidewalk of her home at 4:02 p.m., he came out of the house, grabbed her by the hair of her head, and dragged her into the house, screaming that she was late. Such actions make it almost too dangerous to go visit friends at all. The plan is to make it so, and thus she stays home, alone.

The abuser will see most anyone who is supportive of the victim as a threat to his control. If she has male friends then, according to him, they are all trying to get her to cheat on him, and he accuses her daily of doing so. If she has all girl friends, then she must be a lesbian and is cheating on him with another woman. Many clients tell me they gave up trying to have friends because it was just too much hassle. Or, in some instances, the friends gave up on her because it was too difficult or too awkward to be around her as long as she was with him.

Now, if the abuser has friends of his own and they believe he is the nicest guy, then she can be around them all she wants. They will support him and generally say that if there are problems, it must be her fault.

Next, after separating her from her friends, the abuser will try to drive a rift between her and her family. I don't care how close the family unit has been, it will be severely challenged by his actions and tactics. He makes statements such as her parents don't like him or that they are trying to control her. The abuser will take things out of context and twist them to make it look like her parents or siblings are against her or "them" as a couple.

It's pretty "normal" for our families to have issues of one form or another. Some of these are serious and others aren't. Whatever is there, the abuser will seek to use against the partner to destroy her closeness with her family. Oftentimes, this shows up in little comments such as, "Your mother doesn't really like you, huh?" or "I can't believe your sister is holding grudges against you that way," or "Why doesn't your brother like me?" All of these are designed to subtly create cracks that will gradually widen into rifts and doubts. If there is already a major rift between the partner and her family, the abuser will use it over and over again to exploit it and attempt to kill whatever connection there is.

One saving grace I've seen for some clients is that no matter what the abuser tries, their family stayed right beside them and never wavered in their support. When this family unit is strong, many times the abuser's tactics fail and the partner survives in a healthy way.

Another element here is HIS family. If there are members of his family who say he can do no wrong and every problem is the partner's fault, she can be around them all she wants. They will always support him and tell her there is something wrong with her. However, if one member of his family knows how he is and can't understand why she's still with him, then she can't be around that person or at least be alone with that person.

I had a client who was married to her abuser for about five years. Every time they went to visit his family, his sister would be there. She knew exactly what he was like and would ask the partner why she was still with her brother, considering how abusive he was. Every time the partner got together with the sister, he would show up, laughing and putting his arm around both of them. He'd say something like, "How y'all doing?" and stay with them until the sister walked away. This way, he could keep his partner from getting support from his sister.

The abuser knows where the partner has support. He studies her and listens to her talk about her world. He may not engage in important conversations with her or respond to her feelings all the time, but he listens and learns. This is how he knows where he needs to control her.

For some, it might be church. Many clients I've had were very involved in their church activities. They led meetings or participated in dinners or social events. Perhaps they led children's groups or other functions. What I've seen happen in these situations is that the abuser will get involved in the church as well. He then begins to spread innocent tales about his partner and hint at problems he's having with her. He plays the victim and relates to folks that he's not sure what to do about his partner and how she treats him.

When she eventually hears about these things, because someone comes to her to offer help or to tell her she really needs to be a better partner, she gets upset or reacts, and then they all look at her and figure he must be telling the truth. They can see how upset she is and he plays into that, saying, "You see what I have to live with? I just don't know what to do."

If he works it right, she eventually leaves the church because she feels judged and looked at "funny," as one client put it. Frustration and anger sets in, and she turns to her partner for support. He plays the innocent one who can't understand why these people were such hypocrites, and they decide to leave the church. He's won and she has lost that form of support. If she thinks about going to another church, he reminds her of what happened the last time.

One client was being verbally abused for a long time, before one Friday night, he yanked her hair and pinned her against the wall. He yelled in her face so loudly she thought she'd go deaf. He left the next morning, saying he'd be gone for a while. She was relieved and tried to figure out what she was going to do. She decided to go to her parents and then maybe ask the pastor of her church for support and help in making some tough decisions. Before she could leave that Saturday afternoon, there was a knock at the door. It was the pastor, with her husband standing sheepishly behind him. She welcomed him in, feeling glad that they could talk together. Before she could address anything, even before she could offer him something to drink, the pastor spoke and said, "I've heard some very disturbing things from your husband, and I'm very concerned about you."

"What did he tell you?" she asked.

"He's told me all about your anger problem and how you've abused and controlled him. He told me about last night and how scared he is for you. He wants you to get help so you two can have a peaceful marriage."

She looked at the pastor with disbelief. She couldn't understand. How was he so easily swayed by her abuser? No matter how she addressed it, he persisted that she obviously needed help for her anger, and her denial just made it worse. All the while, she could see her husband standing behind the pastor with this sly grin on his face.

She left that church and she left her husband. Her parents were more supportive, and she eventually found another church. The last time I spoke with her, she was very happy and enjoying her independent lifestyle. However, she still was processing her amazement at how quickly her abuser convinced the pastor that she was the problem.

I've known clients who have actually been dismissed by their church from all responsibilities with the congregation because they filed for divorce from abusive partners. The abusers were "men of God" and taught Sunday school and prayed with everybody. I've had over a dozen clients whose abusers were avid Promise Keepers, which is a Christian men's group. I have nothing against the group or any other church or church group. My point is that just because a man or woman is "godly" doesn't mean they are loving and kind.

In fact, I've had several clients whose abusive partners were pastors. It is one of my top four categories of the worst abusers. I generally regard the four worst categories to be doctors, attorneys, law enforcement officers, and then pastors. All four are positions of power and are looked at by the community-at-large as being educated and "good people." The abusers in these categories, whether men or women, are master manipulators and move several steps ahead of their partners in controlling people's viewpoints of the situations they find themselves in. The challenges these victims face in getting away are extremely difficult.

Other areas of support that victims have might be social groups, girlfriends, knitting groups, and exercise groups. The abuser will work to separate her from any and all of these, using various tactics. Lies, innuendo, false accusations, and crazy-making all work to create rifts and divisions and eventually to isolate the victim so she has no one to turn to for support, except her abusive partner.

Emotional Rifts

As you can imagine, such manipulations leave the partner emotionally scarred. Some of these lost connections may be ties the partner has had for years. Grade-school friends who lose touch because it's just too difficult to be around her. Her closest confidant no longer calls because he answers the phone and says something rude every time. Her girlfriends don't even bother to ask her to join them because they know either he won't let her go or, if she does go, then he will be calling her constantly and making it generally miserable for everyone.

Another aspect of this dynamic is if she has left him before and told everyone about how controlling he is, he then swings back to being a nice guy and asks her to come back. She has a vested interest in the relationship she's worked so hard to make work, she hears him saying all the things she's wanted him to say, and so she returns. Her family and friends all scream, "NO," but she goes back.

Once she's back, eventually he returns to the way he was, and usually worse. She leaves again and goes back to her family and friends. The problem now is that they don't open their hearts like they did before. They're not as supportive as before, and she is perplexed by it. Sure enough, he swings into the "nice guy" and pleads for her to return. She thinks about going back, and her family accuses her of being crazy or says, "You must like being abused." They ridicule her and even threaten her if she decides to go back. This may be driven by their fear for her safety, which turns to anger in their frustration. However, all she hears is they don't want her around, and they think she's crazy.

Oftentimes, when the abuser is being the "sweetheart," the victim hears statements like, "No one loves me like you do," or "I can't live without you," or "How can you give up on us after all we've been through?" Since family and friends aren't as supportive, she turns back to him with a misguided belief that this time he's really changed. When she goes, her family and friends suffer even more and are hurt even deeper. If she tells him that they didn't treat her right, he is quick to play on this and tells her they really don't love her and are all mean to her. He's got her again and will swing back to the old self sooner or later, and usually it will be worse than before.

Does she leave again? I've known of families who told their abused daughter, "No, you can't come here." Friends tell them they're too busy to help. The victim is alone—just where the abuser wants her.

This is where agencies like the Marjaree Mason Center and others come to the rescue many times. They open their doors and take people in to provide shelter, food, support, counseling, and a chance to breathe without being judged.

In all of this, however, it is so important to recognize how emotionally scarred these victims are. These wounds are deep, and they are badly bruised. So many clients tell me stories of attacks, and about injuries that have healed, but they all agree that the worst is the verbal, mental, and emotional beatings they take. The loss of family and friends, the grieving, takes a long, long time to heal.

I've seen families reunited and even friendships restored. These are wonderful experiences. However, in so many instances, there are friendships that are lost forever. Clients grieve, learn, and move on.

Accusations

The verbal aspect of this isolation comes in many forms we've already discussed.

One of the most common accusations is that the partner is sexually cheating on him. No matter where she turns for support, he will accuse her of having a relationship with someone. Or perhaps that she's using her so-called friends as a cover for her to be with some other guy.

I've known of clients who stopped getting together with anyone just to prove to they weren't seeing anyone else. The abuser simply accused the partner of meeting "him" some other way. If she's getting together with girlfriends, he accuses her of becoming a lesbian and says she's having the fling with another woman. Or if she's going to school, she's meeting guys there or she's getting an education to leave him or she's accused of thinking she's better than him because she's going to school. It doesn't matter what the victim does or doesn't do, the abuser will believe what he wants and will accuse her of whatever he wants.

The verbal accusations cover a wide range of possibilities. The victim is accused of cheating, lying, scheming, deceiving, and more. The impact is to cause the partner to stop seeing family and friends, stop talking to family and friends. She stops thinking about going out or going to school or going anywhere. She quits her job, she quits school, she quits interacting with others because she knows he will verbally attack and accuse her of one thing or another. So many clients are told, "You're too stupid to go to school," or "Everyone knows you're crazy, they're just laughing at you," or "You're such a weirdo, no one wants to be around you." The "crazy-making" part of all of this is that there will be times when the abuser is being nice and will tell her how impressed he is with her, how smart she is, how well she's doing. This is the dilemma she faces. One minute he's being so sweet and telling her encouraging things, and the next he's putting her down in the worst ways. Welcome to the world of Dr. Jekyll and Mr. Hyde. The victim lives in this world day in and day out and tries so hard to make sense of it.

Chapter Seven

Relationship Manipulations

"Relationship manipulation" is what I call it when the abuser appears to listen intently to what the client feels and thinks. It seems so genuine to the victim but the reality is that it is all manipulation.

Relationship Manipulation

In order for the abuser to effectively control the victim, he needs to know how she thinks. What she is passionate about and what she thinks on a certain subject is important. Not because she is a partner and her thoughts matter and her feelings are of value. He needs to know these things in order to manipulate and control her.

I've heard client after client talk about the beginnings of their relationship and how they would talk for hours and hours. They tell me how their abuser used to listen and ask questions about how they felt. He would seem so interested. Then, a week later or a month down the road, he would complain about how stupid she was to feel that way or say, "Only a dummy would think like that." Always there would be the put-down.

In these situations, most victims try to explain why they think or feel a certain way to prove to their partner that they are right, or just that they're not "dumb." Engaging in a "reasoning" match with an abuser is an exercise in frustration. No matter how effective an argument the victim uses, it won't work. The abuser will still insist that she is wrong, as usual. Even if the discussion comes down to the only possible answer is that she is right, he will change the subject or go off on a tangent about why she chose to use a particular word, questioning what she meant by it. I've never heard of an abuser coming to a point of saying, "You're right and I'm wrong," unless it was for his own manipulative benefit.

Most every true victim I've worked with has a sense of what she feels is a "loving relationship." This usually includes caring about the partner; sharing ideas and thoughts; being intimate mentally, emotionally, spiritually, as well as physically; respecting each other; encouraging each other; and developing trust. All this and more goes into saying "I love you." The problem in an abusive relationship is that the abuser generally has no clue what all that means. His version of a loving relationship is based on power and control. When an abuser says, "I love you," it means, "You are an object I can control." I deliberately use the word "object." The partner is not a woman with thoughts that matter or feelings that are important. Rather, she is an object he controls to do what he wants when he wants her to do it. She is there to take care of him and his world.

The victim listens intently to what he says, though. When she hears those magic words of "I love you," hope springs in her mind and heart, and she has faith that this time he means it. He seems to listen to her, and she hopes that surely he appreciates her now after all she's done for him, just the way he wanted it, too. Her mind races with thoughts of, "How do I keep him interested, how do I keep him happy?" She ponders and memorizes exactly what he says about how he likes things and what pleases him. She puts so much energy into "getting it right."

She never does. As one lady said, "I just tried to make it through the day. And I never did, not once." Psychologically, this becomes devastating. Again and again, she tries. She knows she did it exactly the way he likes it, except now he's changed. Not only is she wrong, he tells her that he never said he liked it this way and she must be going crazy to think he would ever say such a thing.

This sort of experience is all too common in abusive households. It combines with the crazy-making behavior talked about earlier and leaves the client not knowing what to do. Still, every client I've had tells of continuing efforts to please and trying to make things work. She hopes that the next time, she'll get it right. Sometimes, there are occasions when it seems she does. I had a client talk about making a certain meal she knew he liked, and the results were wonderful. He praised her cooking that night and told her how lucky he was to have such a wonderful wife. However, the next time she made the same dish, he exploded and threw it against the wall, dragged her around the dining room, made her clean up the mess, and demanded she make him something else to eat.

There is no certainty, other than to expect the unexpected. In the abusive relationship, there is no trust and no respect. Key elements of a "loving relationship" are missing. The victim catches glimpses of what she thinks is trust or respect, only to have it jerked away on a moment's notice. This leaves her psychologically broken and questioning her own reasoning.

Plays on Emotions

Abusers often are out of touch with their emotions. I've had facilitators of Batterer's Intervention programs tell me that the only emotion a batterer is really in touch with is anger. However, abusers know how their partner's emotions work. They use this to their advantage in the course of manipulating for power and control. What makes her happy? What makes her sad? What buttons do I need to push to get her angry? Abusers are masters at pushing these buttons just the way they want and getting the response they want to suit their purpose.

One client went to a family court mediation session with her abusive husband. Despite there being domestic violence in the relationship, the mediator waived off her request for separate mediation. As the husband talked about how much he loved his wife and how special the children were to him, the client started fuming. He was terribly abusive to her, he totally neglected the children, and here he was "running this line of bull," as she put it to me, past the mediator. What bothered the client even more was that the mediator was buying it. The fact he wasn't involved with the children was an emotional trigger for her, and they had argued about it for months prior to this mediation session. Now he was lying to the mediator about how much he loved his kids and wanted to spend more time with them. When tears came to his eyes, the client said out loud, without meaning to, "Oh my God," in a most disgusted tone.

The mediator turned to her and said, "You seem to have an anger problem, Mom."

My client glanced at her husband across the table and saw him smiling. He had her. He had successfully pushed her buttons to get her angry in front of the mediator.

His response then was, "You see what I have to deal with. I don't know why she has to get so angry with me and the kids."

This play on the victim's emotions is part of the relationship manipulation that abusers do so well. Never underestimate how powerful this tactic is. One of the strongest bonds is between the victim and her family. I've heard victims talk about having strong family ties until they met the abusive partner. Sometimes, he ingratiates himself with her family, and they think he is wonderful. He only shows them that side of himself. When he can, though, he will drop hints that his partner, their daughter, seems to be having problems and is getting upset more often. She seems to be uncertain as to what's right and wrong. He's so concerned.

Then, when he explodes and she runs to her family for help, they ask her what she did to get him so upset. She must have done something. They all know she's been acting strangely lately. She's puzzled and confused. Rather than getting emotional support from them, they question her stability. Oftentimes, she then returns to the abuser, who by now is acting sweet and charming again. The next time she wants to go somewhere for help, she won't trust her family. He's isolated her, as we talked about before, so she has no one else to turn to. She's alone and he has the control.

Many of the things discussed earlier in the Tools of Abuse chart apply to the emotional abuse I'm describing here, such as the victim's emotional connection with the family pet that gets hit or harmed or yelled at by the abuser. Of course, his anger is blamed on her, and it's her fault the pet is getting abused. The connection she has with the children, her friends, her family, her church, or even her job are all fair targets for his manipulations.

Sounds Good

So often the victim is duped into believing the abuser is really interested in her. Many times, a client has told me she was convinced that this time he was genuinely enthralled with what she was doing.

"He asked me all kinds of questions," one lady said so excitedly. "He told me how great it was that I was getting involved in our son's classroom and wanted to know all about what I would be doing! He's really glad I'm involved!"

About a month later, he was ranting and raving that she was having an affair with the female teacher in her son's class. He was convinced it was all a ploy on her part to spend time with her lover. No matter how much she tried to convince him otherwise, he still accused her. When she pointed out all the excitement he had had at the beginning of her working there, he said he knew then that she was cheating but just wanted to see how far she would go with it. It was all her fault they were having problems now, and he should have stopped it then at the start. Obviously, much to her son's disappointment, she stopped working in his class.

Over and over again, I've heard how victims have been thrilled to hear their abusive partner seem interested in them or what they're doing or in the children, only to later have it all crushed, with her to blame.

"Why do you consult their words
when it's not their mouths that speak?"

Rousseau

Chapter Eight

Eventual Outcomes

In the chart, I've listed three main outcomes of this psychological, emotional, and verbal abuse. I want to take a moment to explain them here.

Learned Helplessness

This is a mental state in which the client believes she is helpless and can never get it right. She knows she cannot change the situation and she cannot escape, so she simply gives up mentally. This is a numbing sensation and what I've described as having her mind "shrink-wrapped in plastic." She's basically given up on her dreams and hopes, and accepts that he is the "lord of the castle" and she is the servant. This victim usually can be seen walking with her eyes down to the ground so as not to accidentally make eye contact with anyone. She knows exactly how long it takes to get to the store, run directly to what she needs, buy it in the fastest line possible, and return home in the shortest amount of time. If something goes wrong in her efforts, she knows what to expect and accepts it willingly.

Earlier-generation victims are often in this state of mind. You hear it in their words to their daughters when they come to them for help.

"You have to just live with it. Your father beat me, and I took it and I'm still with him. What did you do to upset him anyway? You should know better than to do whatever you did this time."

The victim has a general feeling that nothing will ever work for her and that it's all her fault, just like he keeps telling her. Some victims who have tried to get away only to be re-victimized by others, including those she turns to for help, return to the abuser with a renewed sense of "learned helplessness." They start accepting the situation and believe it will never get any better. He has all the power and control, and she'll never be free of him.

Emotional Numbness

Sometimes, I have worked with clients who are totally emotionally numb. They describe times past when they were excited by things or enjoyed things, but their descriptions of these times are in a monotone. It's almost like they are describing a dull and boring movie. They can't seem to generate any enthusiasm for anything, including their relationship and their family. They are walking and talking, but inside they are gone already. This state of mind comes with the learned helplessness.

One of the first signs I watch for to know when a client is beginning to recover is if they come in to the session and they are angry. The angrier they are, the better (within reason, of course).

I had a client once who would describe some very abusive behavior by her partner, but it was all told with no emotion whatsoever. We might as well have been watching paint dry for all the lack of emotion in her voice and in her life. Then one day, she barely got in my door and said, "I'm done!"

"Done with what?" I asked.

"I'm done, I'm done, I mean I'm done!" she exclaimed with each phrase coming louder and louder. She proceeded to vehemently describe things that had happened just that morning before coming in to the session. She had argued with her abusive husband and had had it with all of the abuse. This woman was coming alive again and feeling her emotions. The next challenge was to channel all the rage energy in a healthy way, which we were able to do. The thing is that she came alive and changed that numbness into a vibrant, healthy emotional life again.

I have found that anger is one of the first emotions to come alive for the recovering victim. Having someone listen to them and validate their experience is like fresh water on a dying plant. They will come alive, but at first you might get thorns rather than flowers. There is usually so much anger buried down inside that it has turned to rage. Tapping into this can be a bit dangerous if it all comes out at once. Whether as a family member, friend, or therapist working with the victim, I recommend real sensitivity here to "control" the release of this rage so it can be done in a healthy, healing way.

Another thing I look for from clients is a statement such as, "I forgot how much I used to enjoy doing such and such." They begin to get back in touch with who they are or who they used to be. This is where the flowers come out and the thorns go away, to some degree. It is so exciting to see them come alive. At the same time, if they are still with their abuser or still involved with him in some way, this can be a very threatening and dangerous time for her. The abuser will feel threatened by her changes and will react. Safety planning is very important here (I describe safety planning in Chapter 14).

Verbal Acceptance

In this outcome of the abuse, the victim verbally accepts that everything is her fault. She will blame herself for everything and claim that the only reason he went crazy on her was because she did something or forgot to do something, or she said something when she knew she shouldn't have said it, and so on. The list goes on and on. In some client sessions, I've said, "OK, it's all your fault. Now what are you going to do about it?"

Some abusers will use Bible scriptures or the Koran or other scripture book to show the client how evil she is and that everything is her fault because she's not doing what God wants her to do. In this case, she will tell me that all the problems the family is facing are because she's so ungodly. "God is judging me, and our problems are all my fault." Trust me, I am not making this up. These are things I've heard from clients.

Many times, this part of the outcome of abuse will arise when the abuser has been arrested for some act of violence and the victim is called upon to testify as to what happened. She takes the full blame for everything and states that it was all her fault. When challenged with what was given in the police report at the time of the incident, she will now say that she never said those things and that the police were wrong for arresting him, even going so far as to say they should have arrested her.

Summation

The overall outcome of these various forms of abuse is that the abuser has complete control over the victim. It is this psychological, emotional, and verbal abuse that is the worst part of an abusive relationship. The physical is bad, indeed horrible, but the worst, according to clients, is the non-physical abuse. I hope you, the reader, have caught a glimpse of the world the victim lives in day in and day out. These tactics and tools of abuse operate all day and all night. Whether there are physical bruises or not, the victim is in pain. Whether the abuser is with the victim or away from her, the thoughts, emotions, and sounds of his voice still haunt her. Even when she's gotten away and hasn't seen him in years, they still play out in her mind and in her heart. His words, his looks and gestures, even his laughing at her, bruise her deeply inside both at the moment and for months and years to come. It takes a long time to recover from such things. Her sense of trust is shattered. Future relationships are uncertain.

I believe one of the worst consequences of this abuse is that the client loses herself. She has no idea who she is or what she wants anymore. It is very common to hear, "I don't know," when I ask a new client, "Who are you?" They are quick to confess they've lost themselves and are so confused.

I ask clients some pretty simple questions early on in sessions. "What is your favorite color?" "What's your favorite food?" I sometimes put to them a scenario in which I ask, "If you were going out for dinner, and money was no object, where would you go to eat and what would you order?" You would be surprised how many times I'm told, "I don't know. I haven't been anywhere in so long, all I know is fast food." But if I ask them what their abuser's favorite color is or what his favorite food is, they can answer in a second. They know him, or they think they do, because he can change faster than they can keep up.

One of the greatest rewards in doing the work I do is seeing the victim turn into a survivor. To have a client come in and tell me about something they did just for themselves and say it with a huge smile on their face is so great. One lady went to the beach by herself. She'd never been allowed to go, ever. Imagine living in California for years and not being allowed to go to the beach. Her abuser kept her under lock and key and very isolated. She got away from him, finally. One of her greatest desires was to go to the beach, gather seashells, run in the surf, and play like a little kid. Eventually, she did just that! She related to me how much fun she had and then presented me with a little bottle full of sand and shells as a thank you. I keep it on the table in my office and look at it every day. I've told others about her experience as an encouragement that they, too, can make it. Hearing this and other stories from clients who have rediscovered themselves is simply wonderful. I tell people that when I hear these success stories, "I'm good for another hundred thousand miles!"

Another aspect of the survivor, as I tell clients, is they have a story to tell and others to help. I tell them to not be surprised if, somewhere down the road, they have someone come up to them and relate their story of being abused, looking for help. I've seen it happen again and again. The survivor feels so empowered to help the victim before them. No, they can't, or shouldn't, tell the victim what to do, but rather the survivor can be there for support as they figure out for themselves what to do.

I received a call once from a lady, asking if I had an opening that afternoon to see a friend of hers. I said yes and inquired what it was about. She told me that this friend was a co-worker who was involved in a seriously abusive relationship and she was getting her help. I told her to have the lady call me for the appointment.

"No," she replied. "I have her in hiding. I'll bring her to you."

They came that afternoon and it was the beginning of over a year's worth of work and eventual success for this lady trapped in abuse. Her abuser was eventually sent to prison for threatening to kill her and committing several violent acts against her property and towards her.

About eight months or so after we stopped sessions and she was moving on with her life, she called me. "Do you remember how we met?" she asked.

I related the story of her co-worker calling me and our eventual get-together.

"Well," she said, "now it's my turn! I have this friend I work with who needs help."

She found herself being called on to help someone else caught in abuse, and she was responding with her own experience and desire to reach out to someone else in need.

Family, friends, loved ones of those caught in abusive relationships, I hope you have a better understanding of what they are going through and, with that understanding, are better able to support them to become survivors themselves.

Survivor's Corner

The Discomfort of Changing "Normal"

No matter how much you want to change, the world around you will try to stop it. You'll even try to stop it yourself. When things get out of balance, the natural tendency is to try to get them back in balance. That means when "normal" means a balance between tension and fighting and fear of the unknown, the natural tendency when you're getting out of that "normal" state is to get back into it. We are comfortable in our misery sometimes, and we will try to stay comfortable. It's what we're used to.

Your family will say, "You're different!" or "What's happening to you?" while you're seeing in yourself changes for the better. Yes, you're different. Maybe you're happy for a change. Maybe you're relaxed once in a while. Maybe you're enjoying something for the first time in months or years. You ARE different. You're changing. You're growing. You're getting better.

Months after I filed for divorce and "the Beast" began to settle into his own new life and stopped harassing mine, I began to change. I accidentally had fun. I got a few new friends. I went with them to ball games and a fundraising function. I found I could laugh again.

My daughter didn't like this at first. She's the first one who said, "You're so different, Mom. What's the matter with you?"

"Yes," I said. "I'm different. I'm having fun. I'm not afraid all the time. I'm starting to enjoy my life again."

My best friend saw the changes too, and she didn't like it. She said, "When you were with 'the Beast,' you weren't like this. You were different. I just can't handle this."

What in the world was she talking about? Couldn't she hear herself say that I'm different now? What a blessing! Thank you for noticing! What a compliment to me!

Some people just can't handle the change. They, too, are comfortable in the misery—for now.

To bad for them. I'm moving on!

Keli

When it becomes more difficult to suffer than to change,

You will change.

Anonymous

Chapter Nine

The Cycle of Respect

In looking at the nature of the tools of abuse in the previous chapters, we've gained some understanding of how the victim is psychologically, emotionally, and verbally damaged. We already understand the physical abuse that a victim goes through. Now, I'd like to look at how the relationship cycles through phases that make it "addicting" and almost impossible to leave.

I have included in this and the next chapter two charts showing the cycling of two types of relationships. One is healthy, and one is abusive. I refer to one as the Cycle of Respect and the other as the Cycle of Abuse. In my work with clients, as well as in my own life, I've observed that all relationships cycle. It is the nature of us as humans and how we relate to others. Even the healthiest of relationships is not always a world where "life is wonderful all the time." Indeed, it appears to me there are at least three basic phases that all relationships go through. However, in looking at these two charts it is clear the relationships they describe are vastly different. In the following pages I will attempt to clarify what I mean.

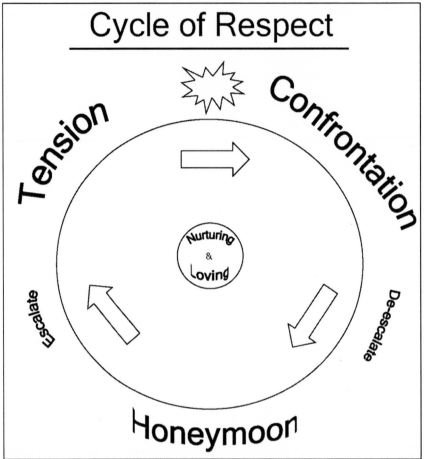

Cycle of Respect

Tension

Confrontation

Escalate

Nurturing & Loving

De-escalate

Honeymoon

<u>Honeymoon</u>: In a healthy, respectful relationship the honeymoon phase is <u>genuine</u>. It's been called "peaches and cream" time. There is mental, emotional, physical intimacy that is genuinely nurturing and caring. The relationship is strong and loving.
<u>Tension</u>: Any relationship has its tension phase. One or the other partner says something or does something and it annoys the other person. There is tension, irritation. Responses to simple questions become short, terse. You might feel like you're walking in a minefield you didn't know was there. Sooner, rather than later, hopefully, it builds until the partners have to talk it out.
<u>Confrontation</u>: "First we cry, then we trust." This is the crying part. This is where the relationship really grows. The cause of the irritation comes out. Both partners talk it out, genuinely listen to each other and accept each other's thoughts and ideas. I didn't say "agree with" but "accept" - there's a difference. Partners agree to work together on things. The next honeymoon stage is now even more intimate because the partners know more about each other than they did before.
<u>Result</u>: As this cycle goes around longer it builds intimacy, trust, and respect. True love-making.

I believe it is the nature of all things to cycle. The belief that the ending of something is merely the beginning of something else strikes a chord inside of me that generates hope. Potentially (and hopefully), each time we go through the cycle, things should get better, we learn more, we apply what we learn, and things improve.

Cycle of Respect

In the Cycle of Respect, things can go this way. In the cycle of relationships, two people come together to enjoy common goals, common interests, common dreams. At the same time, there are differences between them, and yet those differences, in a healthy relationship, are accepted and even nurtured. These differences are not viewed as threatening but rather as elements that help the two people enjoy their diversity. It creates newness and learning about things that challenge us. Many say it is the diversity that keeps everything fresh in a relationship. No, not always smooth, but fresh and rewarding.

So how does this growth happen? How do we reap these rewards in a healthy relationship? It's not because everything goes along beautifully all the time, but rather it's the healthy handling of the challenges we face that brings us together, closer than ever.

In looking at the Cycle of Respect, we see three distinct phases: honeymoon, tension, and confrontation. Let's break these phases down a bit and see what each is like, or should be like.

One challenge I put to the reader at this point is to stop and consider what "honeymoon," "tension," and "confrontation" means to you. Each of us is different. What you bring with you into a relationship is different from what I bring. Your life has been different from mine, or your partner's. Your life experiences are perhaps vastly different. Your highs and your lows may be much higher or much lower than your partner's. Or maybe you don't think you've had much variation in your life. Maybe things have always gone pretty "normal" for you. So what do you bring to your own relationships with others, particularly an intimate partner?

Did you experiment with drugs or alcohol? Maybe you did more than experiment. Do you have children from previous relationships? Maybe you have no children, and maybe you have no previous relationships. What jobs have you had? What education do you have? What were your parents like? What was it like growing up in your house? How does that differ from how your partner grew up? Are you an only child, or maybe you have ten brothers and sisters? The list goes on, and the variations are endless. These are all important elements to consider, though, in looking at our relationships with others, particularly the intimate relationship with a partner.

What does tension feel like to you? Trust me that it is different for many folks. Some are so used to it as part of their daily lives they don't recognize it as "bad" or even uncomfortable. In fact, some are more uncomfortable during times of calm. One client made the statement about her partner that "the only time he seems at peace is when there is drama in the house." So think about what that is like for you, and then consider what it is like for your partner. The lady I described earlier in the book who told her boyfriend, who wouldn't engage in quarreling with her, "I know you don't love me because you won't fight with me" was so used to fighting as part of a "loving relationship" that she didn't know what to do with peace and quiet. Yet her boyfriend was very different and didn't want to engage in senseless arguments. So these standards are different for each of us.

What does confrontation mean to you? I used to think that confrontation meant arguing and fighting and yelling. My own therapist taught me a valuable lesson on this subject years ago. I was telling her about a job interview I went to in which the interviewer asked me a question about the differences between two job descriptions. I had answered him and then at the end of the interview, he asked me if I had any questions for him. I said yes and asked, "So what do *you* think is the difference between the two jobs?"

As I related this to my therapist, she laughed and said, "Bob, I thought you didn't like confrontation."

I looked at her with a puzzled look on my face.

"You couldn't have been more confrontational to him than that. I hope you weren't holding your breath on getting that job," she said. We discussed then what confrontation really is. It can be done in a whisper. In fact, I think confrontation is actually done more powerfully in a whisper than in yelling. It hits harder and deeper if done softer. We're used to people yelling but not to them whispering.

However, before I get too far ahead of myself here, let's get back to the honeymoon phase and examine that.

Honeymoon Phase

The honeymoon phase is what one friend of mine calls "peaches and cream" time. Everyone is in love, and things are going great. All relationships have this phase. Partners are on their best behavior. Everyone seems to be listening to each other and caring about each other. All is right with the world. It's a fun time for all parties involved.

This is the phase where all relationships start. There is a sense of newness here and freshness. One elderly lady described it as "renewal time" for her and her husband of many years. She said that each time they entered this phase, it was like a recommitment to each other to living their lives together.

If the cycle has gone around a few times and a couple is entering this phase again, then, in a healthy relationship, there is that renewed commitment and a sense of being more intimate than ever before. Indeed, the mental and emotional intimacy has grown deeper, and usually that carries a sense of closer physical intimacy as well. We feel accepted by our partner, respected, and there is more trust.

However, the honeymoon phase doesn't last forever. The first problem here is that we are humans. As humans, we don't always agree, and so sooner or later, someone does something or says something and the partner doesn't like it. There is a miscommunication or a misunderstanding of words. Remember, because our backgrounds are different, we can have totally different meanings in the words we use. Perhaps one has done something that, to them, seems totally innocent but the partner takes offense to it. Whatever the reason or trigger, the relationship swings into the tension phase, or as one client put it to me one day, "We're not in Kansas anymore, Toto!"

Tension Phase

So what is a tension phase to you? We've all been there from time to time. Things are now uncomfortable. What seemed to be so easy a few days ago, or a few hours ago, or even a few minutes ago, now seems tense and difficult. Now there are obviously hurt feelings.

I say obviously, but it may not be so obvious to both parties. Sometimes, it takes awhile for the other partner to catch on. There are certain characteristics to the tension phase, though, and sooner or later it becomes clear to all involved that there are problems afoot. One of those characteristics can be avoidance, such that the one who is hurt stays clear of the other. Or, perhaps the one who did the hurting, whether accidentally or otherwise, can feel the awkwardness and chooses to stay clear of the discomfort, more than likely hoping it will all go away. There is usually terseness in words used or the tone of conversations. Whereas before it was, "How are you doing?" and the reply was, "Fine, doing good, what are you up to?" now it's, "How are you doing?" followed by a grunt or an "OK" and that's it. Usually about here, you can cut the tension with a knife. Still there is the "cold shoulder" effect, being quick to ridicule or snap at the slightest issue or misstep. Rather than a welcome home kiss, there is a turn of the cheek or nothing at all.

We all can read body language. Some are better than others at this. However, we all know the body language of our partners. There are always clear signs here that one or the other isn't happy or is tense and irritable.

So what is going on during this phase? The main issue is that one person's boundaries have been violated, and therefore they are angry. Anger is not bad. It's a perfectly great human emotion. It is energy, and we simply need to learn how to handle that energy in positive, constructive ways. In my understanding, which, frankly, is based on me and my own observations, anger tells us we've been violated. It's a secondary emotion, meaning it doesn't exist on its own but rather is generated by something else. It is generated by our boundary, of one type or another, being violated by others.

I have an exercise I do with clients from time to time. I have them stand up, and I stand a few feet away. In this country, we are comfortable standing about three to four feet from each other as we talk or interact.

I address that comfort zone with the client and tell them I am going to step closer to them. I want them to tell me when I am "too close." As I take the step, they are usually quick to react. I am very careful not to touch the client and generally never get closer than a foot or so away. (Only a couple of times have I gotten so close that I was the one who was so uncomfortable I had to stop the exercise. I found it interesting that both of those clients who had no sense of my being too close had been severely sexually abused as children.)

So to continue with the exercise, when the client tells me I am too close, I stand there for a few seconds, asking them to describe what they feel. They usually describe a tension in the chest or shoulders. That, I feel, is a rudimentary form of anger. It is there to tell the brain, "Hey, I'm being violated here!" In this case, it's a violation of our body space. I will step away from the client and ask them if they still feel that feeling. Every time I ask, they say, "No," because the violation has ceased. I step away and the feeling stops. As I step towards them again, it is there again. It's automatic; they don't have to do anything to create it or stop it. It's simply there. I explain that this is how we are as humans. Sometimes, I will turn the client around and tell them to pretend they are in line at a fast food place or wherever they would be standing in line. I then walk up right behind them, as some folks do in lines. Every single time, I get a reaction of the client moving away, or off to the side, and they laugh nervously. I want to see that reaction, because it is a clear sense of boundaries. We've all experienced this.

I tell the story of a friend of mine named Bruce. Bruce is a big guy. He's about six foot, five inches and all of 375 pounds. He speaks in a deep voice and is basically a bear of a man. One of the nicest guys you'd ever want to meet. We were in line at a fast food place one night, and I was at the counter ordering. Bruce was behind me, waiting. Evidently, a gentleman walked up behind Bruce and was standing pretty close, as was the rest of the line behind him. I overheard Bruce turn to this guy and, looking down at him, say in that deep bear voice, "I can't tell if it's my toes or your toes I'm feeling in my shoes. You wanna back up a bit?"

The man smiled sheepishly, nodded, and the whole line backed up about three feet. I smile as I recall the incident because it was a clear statement of boundaries on Bruce's part.

After I've gone through the exercise I mentioned above, we sit down and I tell them to be aware of that same feeling as I say, "You sure are stupid" or "You sure look ugly today." They know I don't mean it, but they still feel the reaction. It's automatic.

We react when we are violated. Whether physically, psychologically, or emotionally, we react. We don't have to do anything about it, and we can even bury it or ignore it, but it's there and needs to be addressed. We do have options here. However, there are consequences to these options. If we run from the reaction, we violate ourselves, and that generates its own anger, thus making things worse inside. We can blame ourselves for it all, and indeed, there needs to be personal accounting in any of this, but if we take on all the blame and it's not ours to take, then we violate ourselves again. We can also blame everyone else for it all. We can do this so much that we hurt the other person as well as ourselves, and, again, things get worse.

Another example I use with clients is in describing what I mean by anger being a secondary emotion. I tell the client to imagine the office is filled with smoke. They walk in and find a thick cloud of smoke filling the room. When asked what they will do about it, they describe opening the windows, opening the door, turning on a fan to blow the smoke out of the room. I thought the same when I first was asked what I would do if I walked into a room filled with smoke. My question is, why is there smoke? It's because something's on fire! The carpet, the chair, something is on fire. You can turn on the fan, you can open the doors and windows, and you can stand and wave your arms back and forth. The problem is that until you address what is on fire, you will continue to have smoke. Indeed, if you just address the smoke and pay no attention to the fire, it will eventually consume the room and you with it.

Well, the smoke is secondary to the fire. The fire is generating it. So it is with anger being secondary to whatever violation we have experienced. We can address the anger all day or try to ignore it even, but the fire will consume us if we don't address the boundary violation(s) going on at that moment. How are we being violated? The purpose of the anger is identify that we are violated and look at how. Then it is up to us to draw attention to the boundary violation in a healthy way and look for ways to not have that violation happen again. Thus, the fire is put out and the smoke will cease.

The point at which both partners become aware of the boundary violation and come face to face about it is where the confrontation phase begins.

Confrontation Phase

A confrontation is a coming together with defiance or hostility. Like I said before, this doesn't have to be done in shouting and yelling. It can be just as powerful (and even more so) if done with softness and whispering. So we confront.

One partner says to the other, "Are you mad at me?"

The other says, "Am I mad at you?" with that look that comes with the disbelief that the other partner even had to ask.

It is at this point that couples have to be careful. There can be a serious and very beneficial conversation and dialogue here. Or it can turn ugly: each goes for the other's throat, so to speak, and no one is listening or hearing anything. So, assuming that the conversation is healthy and constructive, why do we address the anger and the violation? What is the motivation? If the one who feels violated is going to express what they've experienced, what are they hoping for?

I believe most folks go about this all wrong. So many times we speak to the person who made us angry, who violated us, so as to convince them not to do it anymore. We tell them how they hurt us so they will stop doing it. However, what control do we really have over them? What can we say or do that will insure they won't do it again? What can we do or say to change their behavior? Nothing. We really, bottom line, have no control over that other person. So no matter what we say, we cannot guarantee that they will hear us and therefore change and never do it again. So why do it? Why address the issue? If we have no power to make that other person change, why say anything?

We do have control here in only one sense: We control ourselves. If my motivation is to speak up for myself, to address my boundaries and stand up for my own "code," so to speak, then the very act of my speaking accomplishes my task, and I am successful. I feel the purpose of the anger is to give energy to the act of standing up for who I am and honoring that "code" in speaking my mind and addressing why I am upset. If I do it for me, then it doesn't matter what the other person, my partner, does or doesn't do. I have accomplished my task successfully. With this as my motivation, I don't have to yell and scream. I don't have to wave my arms or get "crazy." I can make my point to the best of my ability and then watch to see how my partner reacts. I watch, not because my well-being depends on it, but because I want to know if my partner accepts me and respects my boundaries.

Notice I did not say whether my partner agrees with me or not. Agreement is not the outcome I should be looking for. Acceptance is the key. Does my partner accept me for who I am or not? If so, then we are building respect and trust. If not, then the respect breaks down a little bit, and I'm not so sure I can trust my partner to listen the next time something happens and I need to speak my mind or express my feelings. This is the most challenging phase of the cycle and can also be the most rewarding. I love the line from a movie I saw not too long ago in which one person was trying to convince the other to do something. She realized he wasn't buying it and asked, "Don't you trust me?"

His reply was wonderful: "Old proverb says, 'First we cry, then we trust.'" That old proverb beautifully describes the confrontation phase. First we cry through the confrontation and the difficulties of working through it all, and then we trust, as we feel respected and accepted by our partner.

So, let's say we are in a healthy relationship and we've had our tension phase and we're in the confrontation phase, and my partner listens to me and asks questions about why I feel the way I do. She accepts my position as being mine, and she respects that. She might tell me she feels I'm out to lunch and wrong in my thinking but that's OK, she still accepts my thoughts as being mine, and because she loves me, she will be careful not to disrespect me again. That is her choice, and I appreciate her decision. The change she makes has to be made for her and not for me. If she makes the "change" for me, sooner or later we'll be back here in this same spot again. It won't "take."

The only way change can occur is if you do it for yourself by your own choice. It's the same in counseling. If one person decides to change for the sake of the couple, then before long, once the couple is back together, they will revert back to who they were. They have to change for themselves, because they see they need to change. Then it works for them, and for others as a side benefit.

If the confrontation phase has led to an understanding and an acceptance, then growth can occur. There may be apologies offered: "I didn't realize it would bother you so much," or "I'm sorry I hurt you." These are all fine and good. The discussion, the genuine listening and hearing of each other, not just the one offended but each other, and the acceptance lead to an increase in respect and trust. This then leads into a new honeymoon phase. The two are closer than ever before. There is a new deeper level of intimacy. Mental and emotional intimacy is increased because of the discussion, the learning about each other, and the acceptance.

Now, again because we are human, the cycle will go around and there will be another tension phase and more confrontation phases. But as long as there is good communication and acceptance and respect, the relationship will continue to grow and benefit.

Chapter Ten

The Cycle of Abuse

If the previous chapter was a description of how the Cycle of Respect works and how a healthy relationship is supposed to function, what happens in the Cycle of Abuse? What goes on when things are dysfunctional? Here we will look at that cycle and break it down.

Just as in the Cycle of Respect, this cycle has three phases, identified in the chart as the honeymoon, tension, and explosion or abuse phase. I sometimes refer to the tension phase as an escalation phase. The experiences in each of these phases are very different from what a partner in the Cycle of Respect is experiencing. I will attempt to show this as we go through them.

Honeymoon Phase

The honeymoon phase is where all relationships start. Whether healthy or not, this is the same. Everyone puts their best self forward to try to impress the other person, so they will want to be together. Everyone is nice and considerate and at least somewhat respectful. This is no different in the abusive relationship. I've never had a client tell me that he was a beast on the first date.

Cycle of Abuse

Honeymoon: in an abusive relationship this phase is hollow, a façade, fake. During this phase the victim hears the abuser apologize perhaps, maybe bring flowers or candy, seems to be making-up. However, at the same time he blames the victim for all the problems. It's all her fault.

Tension: "We're not in Kansas anymore, Toto!" This is where the false honeymoon gets rough. The victim is on eggshells and she knows he's moody again. She tries everything to get back to the honeymoon. But nothing works. She can't be perfect enough. She just can't get it right.

Explosion: This phase is the abusive explosion. It might be verbal, psychological, physical or all of the above. The victim tries to reason with the abuser but nothing works. Often times the explosion occurs over something small. The victim can't believe the abuser is upset about it. It's not the victim's fault. The abuser is going to explode no matter what. The victim merely tries to survive.

The longer this cycle goes around the more the abuse escalates and becomes more violent.

Well, I take that back—I have had a couple, but that's not the norm. Usually you won't find a sweeter guy than the abuser on the first dates. I believe there are ways to tell what's really going on and things to watch for in the early goings of a relationship, but, for now, trust me that in the beginnings of an abusive relationship, everything looks and sounds great!

So the initial honeymoon phase in the Cycle of Abuse is usually wonderful. This is where he is being very nice, very sweet, doing things for the partner that no one else would do. I've heard such great reports of long conversations going deep into the night. "He really wants to get to know me. He really is listening to me," I'm told. Remember the old line, "If it sounds too good to be true it usually is"? Well, I've told many clients that if they find some guy and he is just "so perfect," run! We're not that perfect, and sometimes it's all an act.

The problem is that in an abusive relationship, this phase changes. It evolves into a façade, a fake. Some of the words are the same, and they might be exactly what the partner wants to hear, but they don't ring true because of what she's been through. The victim wants to believe them so badly, and they are said with the most sincere tone, and the look in the face is so genuine. Indeed, over time this is part of the "crazy-making" for the victim. "He seems so sincere when he apologizes. How can he keep doing these things to me? He says he wants to change but it's always the same. But he says he's sorry. He really means it. He loves me. But how can he do these things and say these things to someone he loves? He says he loves me." Crazy-making.

In an abusive relationship, this phase might include all manner of ways of apologizing. I've known of abusers who enter this phase after the cycle has spun around and "apologize" with flowers or candy, sincere statements of wanting to get counseling or help in some way, even jewelry and trips. I had a client once who would call me after every explosion and fight. She'd come in for counseling for a few weeks. Then he'd sweep her off her feet again with a major piece of jewelry, such as a diamond necklace or fancy earrings. Once, it was a trip to Hawaii. She'd leave counseling and enjoy her "honeymoon." After about five or six months, she'd call me back and report that he'd beat her up again and she needed help. This went on over a couple of years. She understood she was basically addicted to the honeymoon phase, as she understood it to be. I haven't seen her now for many years.

Oftentimes, there are no apologies here. Many abusers just go on as if nothing happened. I've had so many clients tell me that when they ask him why he exploded and attacked her, he responds by saying, "Let's forget that happened. Let's just go on. Can't you ever let things go? Why do you keep nagging me about it?"

Some abusers do apologize and say, "I'm sorry," after an attack. What I've seen as common is that the "I'm sorry" statement goes something like this: "I'm sorry that I yelled at you and broke things. I know I've got an anger problem. But if you hadn't done what I told you not to do, then none of this would have happened."

This statement appears so sincere and real. However, note what is being said. The only reason anything ever went wrong was because she did what she wasn't supposed to do. So it's all her fault. He's not admitting anything really. Once that word "but" gets injected into the statement, it all changes. The honeymoon statements vary but the blame game is the same. Everything is the victim's fault. The so-called "I'm sorry" is nothing more than a smoke-screen to hide the true meaning of what the abuser is saying—it's all because she didn't do what she was supposed to do, or she did what she wasn't supposed to do, or she said something wrong, or she looked at someone, or she breathed wrong, or—you get the picture.

During the honeymoon phase in the Cycle of Abuse, the abuser is generally nice, and the stress level in the relationship goes down. He plays with the children, they go on trips, and everything seems OK. Indeed, these are the "good times" in the relationship. It doesn't last. This is partly because all relationships cycle and partly because an abusive personality cannot stand for things to go OK for very long. From what I've witnessed and what clients have told me, there always has to be drama. If there is no reason for it, the abuser will create a reason for it. Whatever works for him, there has to be more drama.

One client told me, "It's almost like he's addicted to the chaos!" She had a good point.

Not only does the abuser seem addicted to the chaos and thrive on the drama but he also works hard to engage the victim into the drama and the argument one way or another. In the course of working with victims who are getting out of abusive relationships, one of the hardest things to develop is the ability to disengage from the abuser and not get entangled in the argument and the drama. Getting the victim to engage is one way for the relationship to swing into the next phase.

Tension Phase

In the tension phase of this dysfunctional cycle, the victim can tell that the abuser is not doing well. There are different idiosyncrasies during this time that are particular to each abuser. However, I have found many things are the same.

The victim knows how to read the body language of her partner and can tell quickly that things have changed. Clients tell me of different physical characteristics they've learned to observe. One lady told me that she watched his shoulders. He had a particular way of hunching his shoulders and neck, and she knew she had to be very careful what she said and how she acted. Some tell of their partner's face changing and taking on a certain "look." Another told me she would watch his hands and noted he would start making tight fists when he was getting stressed. None can completely describe this change but the fear in their eyes when they talk about it tells me how real it is for them and how much they dread seeing it.

For some, he becomes moody and does not talk as much. She tries to talk with him more, to talk things out, or she might give him his space and talk with him less. This is a tense time because she's never sure what to say. Many clients tell me of trying to talk things out, and he will suddenly focus on a particular word she used and go off on her for using that word. He wants to know what she meant by using that word. "Why did you say that?" or "What are you really trying to say?" The abuser can become defensive and argumentative very quickly. The victim usually is left wondering what she did or said and why it upset him so much. She finds herself afraid to say anything. However, this can backfire when he demands to know why she's not talking. "What are you trying to hide?" he demands. She's damned if she talks and damned if she keeps quiet. It truly is a no-win scenario.

She might try to give him more time playing with the children or she might keep the children occupied with other things while he's around so as not to disturb him. She tries to cook his favorite foods or keep the house extra clean and organized. She offers more sex or tries to be "better" in bed. She wracks her brain to make sure she remembers all the things he's told her he wants and how he wants it. She strives to be perfect in order to please him and somehow get back to the honeymoon phase.

The tension phase is just that: tense. However, in a healthy relationship there is a trust that eventually things will get worked out and a better understanding will be there for the couple. In an abusive relationship, there is no such trust. The victim knows that an explosion is coming, sooner or later, and she wonders if it will be verbal, physical, or both.

No matter how hard the victim tries to keep things right and "perfect," it never works. This is partly due to the nature of all relationships to cycle. However, mostly it's due to the fact that no matter what she does, he's going to explode. Even if she gets it right all the time and does everything just the way he said he wanted it, he is going to explode. One way I've described it to clients is that the abuser is a powder keg with a fuse and the abuser himself has the matches. He keeps striking them and dropping them on the fuse. Sooner or later, it's going to catch and the keg will explode. No matter what the victim does or doesn't do, look out. It's not so much that the relationship moves into the third phase that's the problem. It's that the third phase in an abusive relationship is so destructive and tears down the "love" she is trying so hard to make successful.

Explosion or Abuse Phase

So we come to the third phase of the Cycle of Abuse. This is the explosion phase, or sometimes called the abuse phase. This is where the name-calling, verbal onslaught takes place. It is also where the physical abuse occurs if there is any. Things get broken here. Sometimes, it's physical things being broken, but all the time it's emotions and hearts that get broken.

So what sets off the explosion? Often, it is what the abuser perceives as an "ego wound." I've heard it described that an abuser has a very fragile personality. He has very low self-esteem and hides it behind a façade of machismo attitude. He has little to no understanding of his emotions or motivations. Many times if an abuser is asked why he hurt his partner, he says something like, "I don't know. I guess she just had it coming." So an "ego wound" to this type of personality often brings about verbal and possibly physical violence.

It's very important to understand that it's what the abuser perceives as an ego wound and not what the victim means in her action or words. I recall one client who was in counseling but was determined to make things work out with her abuser. She knew they were in the tension phase and so set out to change things and get back to the honeymoon. One night, she prepared his favorite dish and set the table with candles. She dressed in his favorite evening gown and was waiting for him when he came home. She said they laughed all through dinner and had such a great time. She was relieved and felt she had been successful. As she was preparing to serve dessert, she walked by him and said, "Honey, I'm going to get a glass of water. Do you want one?"

Now I ask you to stop and put yourself in that situation and consider what's wrong with her question. I know, I can't think of anything wrong with it either. His reply was, "Why do you treat me like a child?" He went on to say, "If I'd wanted a glass of water I would have told you to get me one. But no, b____, you have to treat me like I'm in kindergarten and ask if I want a glass of water? You are so f_____ stupid!"

Things escalated from there, and within a few minutes the table had been turned over, food was all over the walls. He grabbed her by the hair of the head and dragged her around the room, forcing her to clean it up. The cycle had moved into the explosion phase, despite her best efforts. It wasn't her or anything she did or didn't do, it was him. Believe it or not, shortly afterwards, he had spun into the honeymoon phase and was telling her she could clean it all up in the morning. He wanted to go to bed and have sex.

As the abuse continues and the cycle keeps going around in the course of the relationship, this explosion phase becomes more violent. It escalates. At first, it might be only verbal attacks: shouting, yelling in the victim's face. If there is any one word the abuser knows the victim hates to be called above all others, this is where that word gets used on her over and over again. As the cycle keeps going around, this phase begins to include pushing, pulling hair, poking, or maybe a slap along with the verbal attacks. Eventually, if it goes on long enough, it can become hitting, punching, strangulation (choking), and/or pinning the victim against the wall or on the bed, couch, or floor. At some point, weapons get involved. They can be knives, guns, baseball bats, anything that can be used as a weapon to harm or intimidate the victim. This growing violence will usually continue until someone is dead, is in prison, or leaves the relationship.

I've discussed with clients what the first signs were that they were in trouble. I've heard so many different indicators. One lady talked about everything being so perfect until their honeymoon. The day after their wedding, they had argued. She told me that she still doesn't know what the argument was about.

"He just woke up mad, it seemed," she said. "He scared me but I figured it was just the coming down from all the stress of getting married."

That afternoon, they drove to a remote area of the national park they had chosen for their honeymoon. They got out of the car and walked about a quarter mile to a lookout area. He then said he'd forgotten something in the car and was going to go get it. He told her to wait there and he'd be right back. Well, he came back about five hours later. She had been stranded out there, wondering where he was, where he drove off to, what had happened to him. He came back to get her later with no explanation of where he'd gone. Instead, he got mad at her for questioning him.

"Are you hurt?" he asked.

"No, not physically," was her reply, "but I was worried sick! I was scared!"

"Don't be stupid," he said. "God, you are such a c___!"

It was the first time he ever used the "c" word against her. She was shocked because they had talked about the fact she hated that word and felt it was so degrading. He had agreed back then but now he was using it on her. It was the first of many times he would so degrade her.

Their relationship was one that cycled, and eventually the explosion phase became very physical. She recalled being poked in the shoulder a lot. He would pull her hair and scream in her face. Eventually, she managed to get away but not before being punched many times in various parts of her body.

So why did she stay and go through all that? We'll talk more about this in the next chapter, but I want to address part of it here. In abusive relationships, the explosion phase eventually leads into a new honeymoon phase. As I said earlier, though, this version of the honeymoon phase really becomes a trap for the victim. He apologizes, sometimes. If he is one to say, "I'm sorry," she truly believes what he says. Having gone through his wrath and abuse, he is now being kind and sweet, and she wants to believe that things will get better. She wants to believe him when he says he'll get counseling and that he'll never do it again. The truth is, he might truly be sorry but he will do it again, and again. It will get worse until something, or someone, intervenes.

I mentioned that in the previous account, the abuse started when they were on their honeymoon. This is actually quite common. I've seen two times that abuse can "suddenly appear" in a relationship. One is just after getting married. I've had several clients over the years describe sudden verbal, psychological, and physical abuse on their wedding night or during the week after getting married. Mind you, there had been no previous indicators of him being abusive, either in word or act.

I believe there are actually signs and indicators, and work with clients to try to find them as they recall conversations and actions from when the relationship started. Sometimes we find them, and sometimes we don't. However, I do believe they are there. It might be a simple statement made by a relative as in the case of one client who was visiting her new lover's family for the first time. She was talking with his brother at the family barbecue when he walked up to put his arm around her. His brother turned to him and said, "She's really nice. You better treat this one right." She didn't catch it then but she thought about it two weeks later when he had beaten her and then locked her in his bathroom while he went to work. After she escaped by throwing a chair through the bathroom window she called and related the situation to me. She recounted the conversation earlier and now heard it so clearly. "You better treat THIS ONE right." Her question to me was, "How did he treat the others before me?"

Or it might be a comment made as part of a regular conversation. Questions such as "where have you been?" or "what have you been doing" can be seen as innocent or even evidence of genuine concern. But sometimes they are indicators of a controlling personality. One client had been dating a gentleman for only a couple weeks. When she got home after work she received a call from him.

"Where are you?", he asked.

"I'm at home, why?", was her reply.

"You need to call me when you leave work", he said, "I care about you and need to know where you are all the time. I want you to be safe."

This might sound good to some. "See, he really cares about me", I've heard some tell me. But my client recognized it for what it was. She saw he was controlling and trying to make her accountable to him for her every move and action. This after dating for only a couple weeks! She broke off seeing him immediately.

I believe the difference between an innocent comment and a controlling statement/question can be felt in the "gut" by the intended victim. However, we have to be sensitive to this feeling and respond to it effectively. This takes time to develop but I've had several clients describe such situations with great confidence in themselves for "hearing" it and taking care of themselves.

The other time I've heard about is when the victim becomes pregnant. Many clients experience their first physical abuse after announcing to their partner that they are pregnant or during the early months of the pregnancy. My only explanation for this is that the abuser feels threatened by the baby. A baby demands the mother's full attention. That's part of their "job description", I like to say. However, for the abuser, a baby poses a threat because the partner has to take care of the child, and her focus is primarily there and not on him. That's not acceptable for him. Indeed, many clients have referred to the abuser as like having a little child around the house.

It is often said that an abuser has a dual personality—sort of a Dr. Jekyll and Mr. Hyde. During the honeymoon phase, the victim catches glimpses of "Dr. Jekyll," the nice man, the handsome man, the man she fell in love with. It is then that her hopes are rekindled, the hope he will truly change, the hopes that her family, her relationship will survive and work out. And so she holds on and stays (or returns if she has left). However, the more the cycle goes around, the lower her self-esteem goes, the more dependent she becomes, the more she is going to suffer at the hands of "Mr. Hyde," who is the monster of the relationship.

Another point to make here is that as the cycle goes around in an abusive relationship, the faster it seems to cycle. Most victims can tell you about how long the phases are for them. A week, ten days, a month, a few hours: The victim knows. She has to, for her survival sometimes. I've seen a conversation go from the honeymoon through the tension phase and on to an explosion phase and back to the honeymoon, all within a few minutes. Often this occurs when the victim is trying to leave the relationship. An abuser at this time tends to go from extreme to extreme. An example of this is a conversation a client caught on tape one afternoon and played for me the next day during her session. The tape began with her abuser talking.

"Honey, I love you and want you to come back. No one's ever loved me like you do, and I know how special you are," he said.

"No, I'm not getting back with you. You hit me again, and I told you if you did that again I would be gone. I'm gone!" was her reply.

"Why are you being such a hard ass? I told you I was sorry."

"It doesn't matter. Say what you want. I've heard you say it all before."

"You b____! You f_____ b____! You've got someone on the side, don't you? I knew it! I knew it! Who is he? You wait 'til I get my hands on you, you c___! I'm gonna ...!" There was silence on the line for a few seconds.

"I'm sorry, honey," he said. "Please forgive me. I just love you so much."

At this point, she hung up on him and the tape stopped. This type of rapid cycling is indicative of how crazy things can get. Indeed, as I stated earlier in this book, when the victim is trying to leave the relationship is the most dangerous time for her. Something like 70 percent of the victims killed or seriously hurt by their abuser are attacked as they are trying to leave or get away. For the abusive personality, it is the total loss of control, and that is a matter of life and death to the inner self of the abuser. They must regain control one way or another.

Of course, not all abusive relationships end in mayhem. However, I have seen many victim/survivors get away only to have the abuser continue controlling her life through the court system, Child Protective Services (CPS), or other means. One minute he can seem so nice, and the next day she is served with papers or has a knock on the door because some anonymous caller "turned her in" to CPS. The cycle continues.

Chapter Eleven

Why Do Victims Stay?

I believe the statistics indicate that a victim who has left an abusive relationship returns to her abuser anywhere from seven to ten times before she leaves for good, or is killed. This is an astonishing figure. I've had many clients I've worked with make the decision to return to their abuser, or not leave him, in the course of our counseling.

Despite what many people think, there are many and various reasons for this. Why would a victim choose to stay in such a hazardous relationship? In this chapter, I list some of the possible reasons and give insights into how "victims" think or what their reasoning is. Remember from our previous discussions that no two people think alike, and we each have our own points of view. Try to accept and understand what the victim has endured up to the point of deciding the pros and cons of leaving a relationship. It's not as easy as it might seem. Indeed, I've come to the conclusion that leaving an abusive relationship is one of the hardest things a victim can do, and each should be commended for their courage in doing so.

Victim's Childhood Experiences

Back in Chapter 1, I discussed the idea that what we experience in childhood has a tremendous impact on how we are as adults. I used the metaphor of the clipboards in a workshop where we write down, subconsciously, our definitions of things like "loving relationships," "trust," and "anger," based on how we see our primary caregivers act and talk. We carry these definitions into our adolescence and on into adulthood. We think we live our daily lives according to our conscious minds but I believe a large part of our decision-making is based more on the "clipboards" than on what seems "right and wrong" at the time. This is why sometimes we make decisions and act in ways that later our conscious mind looks at it and says, "Why did I do that? What was I thinking???"

If the victim comes from a family where there was a lot of abuse, the abuse she suffers in her current relationship may seem "normal" in that subconscious workshop. This creates quite a conflict for the victim who, on the one hand, wants to get out so badly while, on the other hand, she rationalizes why she should stay. Many of my clients lived in homes where they saw Dad beat Mom on a regular basis. For some, it might have been an aunt and uncle who raised them, or perhaps foster parents. I find, if we examine the relationship between the victim and whoever the primary caregivers were, the victim describes abuse. I know this isn't always the case. I've had clients who say their parents never fought and yet they have been victims of abusive relationships themselves. However, more often than not, the abuse is there. So many come from childhoods where there was fighting and arguing on a daily basis. Screaming and yelling is "normal" to them. Sometimes, the abuse was sibling abuse between brothers and sisters. In such lives, verbal put-downs, threats, and general acts of meanness have become commonplace.

The more a person has grown up in this environment, the more likely they are to "choose" to be that way as an adult. They might become the abuser. It is a learned behavior. They might become the victim. It, too, is learned. The victim learns, in that workshop and written on that clipboard, that abusive behavior is OK. With that frame of mind, things might get so bad she has to step out, but she will return eventually because it's "normal" and "OK." They rationalize that he will change; he said he was sorry; he needs me.

Can this be changed? Oh yes. I've seen many clients rewrite those "clipboards" according to what they want for themselves and what they feel is truly right for them. But first, they have to become aware that the writing is there, that they act a certain way because it is the "normal" thing to do. Once they see that, they can begin to change. However, it is very challenging and something that requires a daily internal focus.

Economic Dependency

As an abuser gains more and more control in the relationship, the victim finds herself becoming more and more dependent economically. The idea of leaving means desperate times financially, and the victim has visions of being homeless, hungry, and totally dependent on others. In addition to this, the victim constantly hears the verbal put-downs the abuser uses incessantly:

"You can't make it on your own."

"No one believes you."

"Everyone knows you're crazy."

"Who would hire you?"

With such comments constantly playing in her mind, coupled with the images of being homeless and dependent, many victims choose to stay and "take it" rather than risk an uncertain future.

If the victim has children, the problems are compounded. In fact, this is more of an unbelievably strong driving force, for most mothers will not risk having their children homeless and without basic creature comforts such as clothing, food, and shelter. Many mothers do not have access to money of their own, may not have jobs, and may not have been in the workforce for many years. I've had clients who go on job interviews and face daunting questions about using computers and other equipment that is commonplace today. They face very challenging obstacles.

If they are looking for the abuser to be removed from the house, they wonder how they will pay the mortgage or the rent. How can they keep up with the utilities and keep gas in the car? How do they provide food for the children? Oftentimes, the abuser has told them that if he leaves, he won't provide them a dime of support. Sure, they might get child support if they file for divorce but that's down the road and not something they are worried about at that moment. With such thoughts and fears, it's easy to see why many victims choose to stay rather than leave. It is the goal of the abuser to keep the victim this dependent on them economically, and it works.

I must say, though, that I've had many clients who have left despite these fears. They have faced the unknown, fully aware of their potential losses. Several have had the surprising experience of finding help in the most unexpected ways. One lady was down to the point of thinking the next call would be the bank telling her they were taking her house. Instead, she called them and explained her situation. The abusive husband had moved out and refused to pay the mortgage or utilities. Three months behind, she called in desperation to see what could be done. After she explained what was going on, the lady at the bank told her to hold on. She came back on a few minutes later and told her not to worry. The bank would go after her husband and do what they had to do to protect her and her children. This gave her time to get a decent-paying job, and she took over the payments on her own several months later. She still lives there today and is doing very well.

Others have had such good experiences as well and have grown stronger for the ordeal of making their own way. There are lots of great success stories out there. But it is so very important for those on the outside to realize how difficult it is to take those first steps. Further, it is important for those still caught in the confines of their relationships to know, it can be done.

Isolation

Remember, from the Tools of Abuse chart shown earlier in this book, one of the abuser's tactics is isolation. Often the victim is not allowed to work outside the home and is kept out of touch from those who might be able to help her. He controls where she goes, whom she talks to, how much time she can spend out of the home or away from him. All of this is meant to keep her out of touch with her family and friends so there is no support from the outside. Combined with the crazy-making put-downs and debasing verbal abuse, generally the victim feels there is no one out there who will support her. No one will understand or believe her. Oftentimes, the victim also has no idea of the services available to her and the children, if she has any. As a result, the outside world can look very bleak and scary, whereas the inside world, although horrible, looks familiar.

This is an area that is so important for those who have loved ones caught in abuse. If they seek to leave, they turn to you for help and understanding. Remember, the abuser has worked hard to drive a rift between you and your loved one. Her mind is filled with the things he has said, the threats he has made, the innuendos, and the abusive put-downs. She probably already feels you don't understand her, you think she's crazy, you hate her and him and everything she's worked so hard to save and make work. You might have been very supportive, and still she acts like you are against her and she doubts your sincerity. Be patient. Be there for her with understanding, support, and healthy communications. Don't judge, don't condemn, and don't tell her she's crazy if she says she still loves him. Listen to her, let her talk without judging. Remember, there is a part of him that is loveable to her: that "nice guy" who she sees every once in a while and who she hopes will want to work on the family as hard as she does, the one she hopes will get counseling or help in some way.

Through your understanding and continued offers to help, the hope is that she knows you are there for her. This gives her the opening she needs and the means of escape.

Fear

By the time most victims give serious thoughts to leaving, the abuser has established quite a foundation of fear. The victim is usually so intimidated by this time and feels so helpless that the slightest difficulty will cause her to rethink leaving or return, if she has left. It is this deep, gut-wrenching fear that causes a victim to say, "It's all my fault," "I caused it," "If only I hadn't done this or that." The victim is usually very justified in feeling so frightened. The abuser threatens and follows through with violence to get revenge if the victim tries to leave. As I've said before, statistically it's proven that the most dangerous time for the victim is when she is trying to get away. This fear becomes multiplied if the victim has children to be concerned about.

Sometimes, the fear isn't that the abuser will strike the victim. Oftentimes, I hear reports that the abuser has told the victim, "If you try to leave me I'll just burn down your parents' house" or "Don't think you can run from me, I know where your sister lives and I'll take her out." He turns the abuse into a threat against the family or against a friend he thinks might help her. I've also had a couple of instances where the abuser threatened to kill the children if she left him. The victim hears these threats repeatedly, and even if she believes only 10 percent of them, it is enough to keep her in his control.

Another threat I've heard used is that even if the abuser is in jail or going to prison, he tells her that his "brothers" in his gang will "take care of her." One client had phone calls from his buddies asking how she was doing, telling her they knew where she had been that day because they were following her for him. They'd call and tell her that he said hello from jail and then they'd hang up. She was in constant fear for her life. Eventually, she managed to escape in the dark of the night with the help of an uncle who lived several hundred miles away. She took only what she could pack in a couple of suitcases. She left the apartment, furniture, and clothes. I haven't seen her since and only hope she is doing well and is enjoying a new life.

To an outsider who doesn't understand the psychological abuse that has gone on, the victim's decision to stay or return can make it appear the victim is "crazy." It can seem like pretty self-destructive behavior. However, the fear factor is very real to her. It's real, intense, and very deep-seated. But she's not crazy. I've talked with some therapists and counselors who say that because a victim decided to go back, she must be "mentally irregular." No, she's not. She's scared. She's been brainwashed, if you will, into believing she can't make it on her own, or that no one will believe her, or she fears she will be hurt or her family might be hurt. There are lots of reasons, and if we were in her shoes, we might return too.

Sometimes, clients are very self-condemning when they've left the relationship and then talk about having had opportunities to leave before but didn't. I always tell them not to be too hard on themselves. The lady who had the chance before probably weighed out her options and decided it was the better part of valor to stay. Sometimes it's for the kid's sake; sometimes fear of what might happen. For whatever the reason, at the time, it seemed the right thing to do.

Learned Helplessness

This is an acquired development within the victim. It occurs as the victim goes through the various stages of the Cycle of Abuse. There are times of danger, but there are also those times of gentleness and goodness. The result is the victim doesn't know what to expect and learns to believe there is nothing she can do to change things. Everything seems out of her control. The longer this goes on, and the more the cycle goes around, the more the motivation to leave diminishes.

The impression I get from clients is that the more this develops, the more the focus becomes mere survival and minimizing whatever injuries might occur. One client told me, "I didn't have time to think about what happened yesterday, and I certainly didn't have time to worry about what might happen tomorrow. I just wanted to make it through the day."

The victim takes on the "victim" mentality, and even when she is successful in changing things, she can't accept it or believe it. Any perceived failure on the part of the "system" such as law enforcement or the courts is accepted as, "Oh well, that's the way it is always with me" or, as one client told me, "I should have known better than to try." Sometimes, this is the motivation behind a victim recanting her testimony in court. She feels the system won't do anything anyway, so why fight it? "It's better to change my statement now and hope he's not too mad when he comes home." If her family has trouble accepting her or working with her, she thinks, "He told me they wouldn't help me and he was right." This takes on an almost fatalistic attitude.

The victim who has become a survivor has had to deal with this attitude and worked to change it. This is no easy task. Trust me! However, I've seen many clients do it and come out stronger than ever. These are the clients I see so often coming face to face with other "victims," and calling on their own life stories, they do more to help them than most therapists can. Their life experiences tell the story and give the hopeful survivor the belief that change is possible and she can have a new life, a life liberated from the abuse. She, too, can be a survivor.

Why We Stayed

Below I have some quotes from victims/survivors. Some of them are my clients and some have been clients of other therapists whom I've met in support groups or at meetings. All of them tell a statement of why they stayed or returned. Read carefully what they say. They've lived it.

"I thought he'd change when he got a job and quit drinking. I really felt things would get better."

"I didn't believe that this was happening. My partner said I was the problem and my friends didn't believe that she was capable of such violence." (This comment was from a lesbian client of mine.)
"I was taught that I should stay married no matter what. I was told I needed a husband, the kids needed a father, and any problems could be worked out if I just tried hard enough."

"He said that if I ever left, he'd find me and kill me, and if he couldn't then he'd just kill himself."

"I didn't ask for help because I felt people would think I was stupid for staying as long as I did. Besides, I considered myself a together, successful person, not battered."

"When she wasn't being abusive, she was very kind and gentle, like the woman I fell in love with."

"I knew he was abusing me but I also knew he was in a lot of pain. He was abused as a child. I wanted to help him. I was sure that with time, I could."

"I had to take care of the children, the household, and even his parents. I didn't have time to worry about my own needs, much less my safety."

"I wanted to get help for us. I wanted him to get help. I wanted my marriage to work!"

"I couldn't leave because it took all the energy I had just to make it through the day."

Chapter Twelve

The Effects of Domestic Violence on Children

"He's such a wonderful father to the kids. He plays with them and spends time with them. He really loves them."

I don't know how many times I've heard these words expressed by domestic violence victims. It is usually followed by, "If he would just get some counseling and help and stop hitting me, then everything would be wonderful."

The truth of the matter is that if he is hitting the victim and obviously, then, verbally and psychologically abusing her, then he is also abusing the children. It doesn't matter how much he plays with them or "loves" them. If there is abuse in the house, the children are traumatized by it.

"Oh, but the kids are never around when he attacks me!" I often tell my clients that the children have a better idea of what's going on in the house between the adults than the adults do. Adults can manipulate ideas and rationalize away the reality of the situation. Children can't! They take it all full force without disguises, without rationalization. They can "feel" the tension and the mistrust. Because they are not the intended victims, they suffer what has been called "incidental abuse," and it has a tremendous impact on them.

Remember earlier in this book, I mentioned that the batterer's idea of a "loving relationship" is the cycle of abuse in which he is nice for a while and then swings around into a tension phase followed by explosion into verbal and/or physical abuse. This is a learned behavior. Where do you think it was learned? The child watches Mom and Dad, or Mom and boyfriend, or Mom and Stepdad, and learns by example. I've also seen the situation where it is Dad who is the victim and the abuser is Stepmom or girlfriend. I've had one client tell me that her abuser's parents were the nicest people in the world and loved each other so much. But when asked about his childhood she said that he was raised more by his paternal grandparents than his mom and stepdad. She related that he told stories of his grandfather beating his grandmother on a regular basis. Suddenly the lights went on inside the client, and she realized where her partner learned to abuse.

"Oh my God," she said. "He's doing the exact same acts to me that he told me about his grandpa doing to his grandma!"

The Clipboard and Learned Behavior

In Chapter 1, I wrote about the clipboard metaphor and that we write down on the different clipboards in our "workshop" the various definitions of various aspects of our lives. We write down what we observe far more than what we hear. Also, it's not according to what is right or wrong but rather what we see. As children, we take it in and write it down. Later in life, that clipboard determines far more of how we act than what we consciously think about. It is unconscious and automatic. It is the same for our children as it was for us. Carry that over to the abusive relationship and see the impact on the child. As the child hears the yelling between his primary caregivers, he writes that down. This is a loving relationship. Yes, it is awful and the child is scared and it is a traumatizing event for him, but he writes it down nevertheless. If it happens on a regular basis and is a part of the relationship he witnesses between his primary caregivers, it goes onto the clipboard as the definition of a loving relationship. This becomes the guideline for him later in life.

Studies show that male children who witness and hear domestic abuse in their household on a regular basis are far more likely to become abusers themselves. Also, if a little girl sees Mom getting beaten, verbally and/or physically, on a regular basis, then she is very likely to become the victim of abuse herself. She might find some nice men in her life but she will tend to leave them for the man, or woman, who will most fit the pattern she saw as a child and become a victim of an abuser. In these situations, invariably they will say how much they hate abusing or being abused but they are following what is written down from childhood, and the inner self, the little boy or little girl inside, says, "What's the problem? I don't know why you're so upset. This is normal. This is what's written down. It's OK."

It's not until they learn about this inner, subconscious guideline that they can rewrite the clipboard according to what they want in a relationship and effectively change their lives. Indeed, by changing their lives, they begin changing what is already written on their own child's clipboard.

Evidence

So what evidence is there that the child is suffering from living in a home where there is abuse? Mind you, the child might not be physically abused, so there are no bruises or cuts or scrapes or outward physical evidence. However, there are definitely psychological indicators and physical actions that indicate that child is all black-and-blue inside.

What I have witnessed is that the child knows, subconsciously, that his world isn't safe. There is fighting, arguing, tension in the house. He is the victim of the cycling relationship too. The child is scared, and this fear usually comes out in the form of anger and acting out. This acting out can be directed at himself or at others, or not necessarily acting out towards anyone else at all. Still, the actions are there, and the words. I remember a client who had gotten away from her abuser and was starting a new life. The abuser had moved several thousand miles away and was no longer a threat. During the time of his absence, her three-year-old little girl had calmed down a lot. While Mom and Dad were still together, the daughter was quite a handful, according to Mom. She would yell and scream, seemingly for no reason. She'd throw things and have tantrums. This little girl had witnessed a lot of abuse between her parents. She had even once been in her mother's arms while Dad was chasing Mom around the house, beating on her if he got close enough. With Dad gone, however, she had calmed down noticeably. Things were going well until one day, when Dad called to yell at Mom about his having to pay child support and other issues. He asked to talk with his daughter and did for a few minutes. According to Mom, who listened in, he told her he loved her and he missed her and hoped to see her again one day soon. That was it, no yelling at her, no threats, just niceties and "sweetness and light," as a friend of mine calls it. The conversation ended, and Mom and daughter went on about their day. Mom was troubled by the call but still enjoyed the rest of the day with her daughter. Later, about 3 a.m., Mom woke up in the dark, hearing strange noises coming from the living room. She got up and fearfully turned on the light to find her daughter sitting in the living room, throwing toys at the wall. She had already gotten a half-gallon of milk and another of orange juice out of the refrigerator and emptied them onto the living room carpet. Talk about acting out! The phone call from earlier in the day was enough to trigger in that little girl all the unsafe feelings all over again. Mom was shocked. Her little girl hadn't done anything like this in many months and never this bad. It took some time to calm her down and reassure her that her world was indeed safe now.

Other children act out by becoming verbally abusive towards whichever parent is the victim of the abuse. One client's two-year-old son would call her a "b____" all the time. He didn't know what that meant but Dad called her that often enough so he picked it up. I had a client once who had left her abuser and was coming in for counseling but would bring her six-year-old son and two-year-old daughter. She would tell them to wait in the waiting room. We'd have the door slightly open so she could hear them interacting. One morning, they were not getting along very well, and the little boy came to the office door and said he couldn't get along with his sister that day. Mom told them to go back to the waiting room and to try to get along. The little boy went but the girl stood there with her hands on her hips, defiantly objecting. When Mom insisted, the little girl turned to her mother and said in a strong, deliberate tone, "F___ you! F___ you! F___ you!"

She then walked back to the waiting room, and Mom sheepishly turned to me and said, "I'm sorry. She learned that from her father, who used to say it just like that to me all the time. I haven't been able to break her of it when she gets this way."

The children learn from what they see and will mimic the acts of the parents, good, bad, or indifferent. And so the acts and attitudes get handed down to the next generation. In this situation, the little girl learned from her father. I've also seen where Mom is the abusive one and the little boy learns from her.

Another client of mine had endured a lot of abuse at the hands of her husband but stayed in the relationship for the sake of the children. She said she felt if she stayed, then she could take care of them because he was one to yell at them a lot and threaten them with beatings. He never did hit them, she said, and so she felt she was protecting them by being there. This went on until one day her young son walked up behind her, slapped her very hard on the arm and shoulder, and said, "Get out of my way, b____!"

The boy proceeded to walk on by without a moment's hesitation. Needless to say, she was in total disbelief of what she had just heard and felt. She indicated that her husband had done the exact same act about two days before but she didn't realize her son had seen it. She found out later when she talked to her son about the incident.

Not all children act out in anger and abusive language like these I've related. Others become quiet, reserved, almost hidden away within themselves. I told the story earlier about the mom whose husband came home with the knife set and proceeded to rub the knife on his wife's chest in front of the kids. He put the knife away and although he never said he would kill Mom with it, the little girl knew what he meant and questioned Mom later and said that if he did kill her, then she'd tell the police how he did it. What a torment to put on that little girl's mind and emotions.

It's important to note here that if you were to see that family outside, they would appear completely "normal." No neighbors knew about this incident, Mom told no one until she told me that day in my office. So behind the smiles and the appearance of happiness, there were several souls battered and bruised mentally and emotionally. This is the side of domestic violence of which most people are unaware—the psychological and emotional abuse that eats away at a person inside while they are smiling outside. This happens to the little ones as well as the adults.

I worked with a little boy once who lived with his mom in the Marjaree Mason Center, a shelter for battered women and their children. In the course of the therapy I did with him, we would play and draw pictures and talk. One day, he drew a picture of his mom and dad out in the vineyards near their home. He was a pretty good artist, and it was clear that Mom was lying down on the ground between the rows of grapevines and Dad was standing over her. I asked this little seven-year-old what he had drawn.

"This is the day I saved my mom's life," he said very matter-of-factly. "Mom and Dad were yelling and went outside and I went looking for them. I found them and Dad was pointing a gun at my mom's head. See?"

He pointed to his drawing of his dad's outstretched arm with a black object in his hand pointed at Mom's head.

"When Dad saw me coming, he put the gun in his back pocket and went away. I saved my mom's life that day."

No matter how you want to avoid it, this is child abuse. No, the child wasn't physically hit or even yelled at. However, the trauma to that little psyche from what he witnessed will live with him for the rest of his life. An even greater concern is that that little one has imprinted on his clipboard that this is a loving relationship. I know, I know, it is so horrific, surely he knows it's not right. Sure he does, but the inner workings of that little self don't go by right and wrong, only what he sees and hears. There were times that Dad could be a lot of fun, and we talked about playing in the park and times he laughed with his dad. Then he'd tell me about how mean Dad could be to Mom. The cycle of abuse is imprinted and I wonder now, so many years later, what he is like with the women in his life and if he has children.

Another incident happened in the childhood of a forty-year-old client I used to have who came to me for her anger issues. She described how she would fly off the handle at the slightest provocation. She was verbally abusing her partner, and the week before she came in, she had struck her during an argument. She wanted this to stop but didn't know what to do. As we talked about her and her life, we went back to childhood. She recounted to me that it was all her fault that the family had broken up. She had never been able to forgive herself for what she'd done. As I probed for more information, she recalled, "I asked my mom to make us pancakes one morning."

I waited for more but she said that that was the reason they broke up.

"How is that?" I asked.

"Well," she said, "I asked Mom to make us pancakes and she said there wasn't enough time. The next thing I remember is Mom and Dad fighting and Dad hitting Mom all over the bedroom. Then he left for work. Mom packed us all up and we went to live in a shelter. That was the last time we were ever together as a family, and it's all my fault because if I hadn't asked Mom to make those stupid pancakes, then we'd all still be together."

"So you blame yourself for the breakup?" I asked.

"Of course I do!" she barked. "It's all my fault. Everything is my fault, always has been."

We went to work on these memories and telling that little girl inside that it wasn't her fault and she didn't do anything wrong. The client began to realize that a majority of her anger was at herself. It had been building over all these years because she blamed herself for everything that went wrong from that day forward. As she released her sense of shame and guilt, she began to feel better about herself. Her anger decreased and her relationship improved dramatically.

What is so important here, and why I share this story, is I want you, the reader, to see the impact of the abuse on that little girl. She had not said anything to anyone about how she thought of that day until in my office. Her mom never knew, her father never knew, her siblings never knew that she blamed herself for the family breakup. As far as she was concerned, for all those years, Mom and Dad fought because she asked Mom to make pancakes. As adults, we know that isn't the case, but to her it was very much the situation. It was this guilt that stirred such self-loathing inside and generated all the anger that was coming out at everyone else, especially her partner.

There are other ways that children who live in abusive households will show their insecurities and fear. They may tend to complain a lot about physical ailments such as headaches and stomach aches. They may act depressed and withdrawn from others, or they might go the opposite direction and be very involved with other kids and act out against them, bully them. There can be eating difficulties, whether eating too little or eating too much. Almost always there are problems with academic work, with abused children failing classes. However, I have also known of a couple of adolescents who excelled in school and got straight A's. They took extra time in school and stayed after class for tutoring they didn't really need, but it kept them out of the house and away from the abuse. One young boy said that focusing on class work and homework helped keep his mind off the yelling and screaming going on at home. Some adolescents show signs of the learned behavior early on, with temper outbursts and aggressiveness towards the opposite sex. Teen dating violence and controlling behavior at school are major red flags and indicators of what's gone on at home. The stress at home can also lead the children to seek "self-medication" just as adults do. This leads to alcohol and substance abuse at early ages. I'm not saying that all such problems indicate that domestic violence is going on in the home. However, such violence and abuse will generate these various symptoms.

Trickle-Down Theory

Another side of this environment is what I call the "trickle-down theory." Dad abuses Mom. Mom isn't able to successfully fight back against Dad, but she is very angry and upset. The abuse then trickles down the chain of the family, and Mom abuses the children. This can be in the form of hitting, yelling, screaming, throwing things at them, or perhaps placing impossible demands on them.

One client I had years ago told of her father abusing her mother. She doesn't remember them hitting each other but she did recall a lot of times when Mom and Dad would yell at each other and cuss each other out. She said Dad was always accusing Mom of cheating on him and Mom was always catching Dad actually cheating on her. It was a lot of mutual verbal abuse. The threats always came from Dad to Mom, however. Dad was always threatening to kill Mom, or according to the client's description, he would take a stance as if to hit her with his closed fist. She never saw him actually hit her, though, and couldn't recall ever seeing any bruises.

This client loved her dad and said he was always nice to her. She felt she was his favorite of all the kids. Her relationship with Mom was quite different. Mom was a tyrant to the client. She remembers her mother yelling at her with the same voice she used on her father, even the same words. She recounted one session that Mom would tell her to go to her room and not move or make a sound. She would go and sit in a chair, motionless. It never worked, though, as Mom would invariably come in, slap her across the face, and yell at her that she'd heard her talking or moving around.

As she became an adolescent, Mom was always accusing her of messing around with boys. Even when the client had no boyfriend and hadn't left the house, Mom would accuse her of having some boy in her room. I found it interesting to learn, in the course of our work, that this client had five children by five different men, and all of them had been very abusive to her. What did her inner description of a loving relationship look like? Where did she learn that? How was she living it out in her life? These were all questions we looked at and worked on. I am happy to report that she became quite a success story. She worked hard on rewriting those inner scripts, and when I last worked with her, she was taking care of her kids, teaching them healthy lifestyles, and determined to take care of herself.

It is so important for clients to look back at their lives and see how the abuse they witnessed and lived through affects them today and how it affects their own children. So many don't see it. They act in ways that seem "normal" and oftentimes are not aware of how they speak to their children, or neglect their children, or even abuse their children. They know they don't hit them, but they are not aware of the serious impact that verbal and emotional abuse can have. However, when they become aware and take the difficult steps to change their own behavior, they are often rewarded with changes in their child's behavior. One mom told me that not only were her daughter's grades going up in school but that she hadn't been sent to detention in many months. She said the shock of her life, though, was the previous week when her daughter made her bed and picked up her room without being asked to do it. The client laughed as she told me and had the biggest smile on her face. She was enjoying the changes.

Listen to the Kids

One other point I want to make here is for the adults to listen to their kids. Like I said before, the children often have a better idea of what's going on than the parents do and often have better insight into how to solve the problems. Children become confused when they see Dad beat Mom or scream at her and then Mom says to them, "Oh, your dad was just upset about some things. It's no big deal."

It is a big deal to the child! They know things aren't right, and their world, as far as they are concerned, isn't safe. They know this internally, and yet here is the parent telling them it's all right. As a result, they are confused, and this leads to an internal struggle that oftentimes comes out as anger.

I've had some children who put voices to their confusion. They are in disbelief as they watch the adults act so childishly. As a result, for some, they stand up to the parents and speak out. Often, this is put down immediately as the child being disobedient or rebellious, but listen to them. Hear what they are saying.

I had a client who had gotten her abuser out of the house but kept letting him come back every other weekend or so. Each time he came back, they'd be happy for a day or two, and then everything would blow up and he would storm around the house, yelling and breaking things. Her six-year-old son would run and hide in his room when the fighting would start. Eventually, it would end when she kicked her abuser out of the house, and she would tell him to leave and not come back. One day, after such an incident and the dad had left, she was walking down the hall in the house and spotted her son standing in the doorway of his room.

"I'm so sorry," she said. "I hate that you have to listen to all that. I just don't know what to do about your father."

"You don't know what to do?" he asked with a stunned look on his face. "Leave him and stop inviting him back in!"

The client was stunned. Her son had a better understand of what to do than she did.

"I don't want you to grow up without your father," she told him.

"I don't want to be around him. He's mean to you and to me. Get rid of him!" These were strong words coming from a six-year-old boy, but it is what my client reported to me. Having met the boy, I can believe that he said these things. He was mature far beyond his years. But it shows that children don't want to live in this abusive environment. It scares them and they don't like it.

So many times, I hear of children telling their parents to stop fighting, stop hurting each other. When one partner is abusive to the other, the kids want it to stop. They suffer the consequences of the parent's actions and, sometimes, inability to act. This happens to children of all ages. Listen to them as they play, listen to them when they talk with each other, listen to them when they talk to you. Hear them.

The Stand-In

Another observation of mine occurs when the abuser leaves the house and is "out of the family" for whatever reason. He might have moved away or might have been put in prison. For whatever reason, there is now a void where the man of the house used to be. What I see happen is that the male child, or sometimes the female, will attempt to assume the leadership role and stand in for Dad. The phenomenon is such that Mom obviously isn't in control because Dad was always dominating her, and now that Dad is gone, it falls on the child to take over. This can include carrying on the abuse. It takes a lot of work on Mom's part to regain control and get the family functioning "normally" again.

One such family was put into this situation when Dad attempted to kill Mom one day. He was taken off to jail and eventually was sentenced to several years in prison. Mom was left to run the family with four children and no job. She was going to have to provide for them all as a single parent. Almost immediately, her older son, who was in his late teens, started yelling at Mom and verbally abusing her. The daughter, who was a couple years younger than her older brother, stood up for Mom and would challenge the brother. They'd fight almost every night, with the son calling her names and threatening to attack her and Mom. Usually this was when the younger son, who was a year or so younger than his sister, would step in and try to mediate the situation to calm everybody down. Things escalated and several times got so out of control that Mom had to call the police. I was working with the youngest of the children, who was about fourteen at the time; one day he said, "Dad went to prison so we could have peace. But there is no peace."

I've seen this scenario play out several times in many families. In this particular family, Mom stayed with it and set healthy boundaries.

The children learned to adjust and respect her discipline. All, that is, except the oldest child. I fear that today he is just as abusive as his father.

Teach by Example and Actions

Particularly when dealing with adolescents and teenagers, teach by example. They watch you like hawks! They see what you do and hear what you say even though you think they don't really notice you anymore and certainly don't listen. They do see and they do hear.

Listen to what they say and how they say it. Use reflective listening skills, where you tell them what you hear them saying and ask if that's what they mean. You'd be surprised how often the words spoken mean something totally different than what you think. Through feedback and patient conversation, you can learn what the teen is thinking and vice versa.

Respect their point of view and don't underestimate the intelligence and insight they have. Like I've said before, often they know more about the situation than you think and have a clearer idea of what to do about it. They may not share it because they figure you won't listen to them or respect their ideas. Show them you care and want to know what they think. Accept it and listen.

In validating their thoughts and words, you can empower them to be a partner in the situation. Yes, they are the children and you are the parent, but they can still feel they have a hand in solving the dilemmas you face together. Provide lots of options and ideas of your own and process together. This way everyone learns. Be patient and supportive in working with your children/adolescents. They may learn at a different speed than you. They may have different fears and problems than you do. Still, encourage, accept, validate, and listen. Let them know that what they feel and say is important.

Survivor's Corner

The Little Girl in Me

The little girl in me said, "He loves you,"
The woman knew better somehow.
The little girl in me said, "You've done this before,"
The woman said, "Get out now."
The little girl in me said, "I'm alone and afraid,"
The woman KNEW she'd be dead.
The little girl in me said, "I've nowhere to go,"
The woman used her head.
The little girl in me said, "People can't know,"
The woman cried out for release.
The little girl in me said, "Someday it will stop,"
The woman said, "Someday I'll find peace."
The little girl in me said, "It's my fault I'm here,"
The woman KNEW it was a lie.
The little girl in me said, "I'll stay 'til it gets better,"
The woman found wings to fly.

Tami

Chapter Thirteen

Re-victimization

This is a chapter I feel I have to include in this book. I write it to prepare those who eventually leave an abusive relationship, to warn them that it's not all smooth sailing once they leave. Most survivors know it will be rough, but they may not expect the challenges to come from those they thought would support them. One client of mine said, "If I'd known it was going to be this hard, I probably wouldn't have left!"

Loved Ones and Friends

Unless loved ones or friends have been in abusive relationships themselves, they may not understand all the victim has been going through. Particularly they don't understand all the "hidden abuse" such as verbal attacks and psychological crazy-making incidents and comments the victim has lived with for months or even years. They may not understand why the victim is so depressed now that she is out of the relationship. She is clear of the abuse, so why isn't she celebrating? I have never had a client celebrate the end of a relationship with an abuser. Not one. Later they talk about being free of the abuse and becoming themselves, but early on they are grieving the loss of what they have struggled so hard to try to make work. This grieving can show up as being sad, irritable, short-tempered. The survivor is often confused when she leaves and fearful about what life will be like now that she is responsible for herself and possibly the kids.

Also, the abuser may still be very much in the picture. I've never known an abuser to just walk away from someone they've controlled. Remember, the cycle keeps going. When the victim leaves, the abuser swings into the honeymoon phase and tries to charm her back. He can sound so convincing, and she hears everything she's wanted to hear. If she hesitates, he can swing through the cycle very quickly and become verbally abusive and then just as fast swing into a new honeymoon. This leaves the victim very confused. I've heard an abuser go from one extreme to another and back in a matter of seconds.

If her loved ones and/or friends are challenging her to "be happy" or "don't be crazy" or asking her, "How could you think that way?" then she might decide he was right, they don't want her around, and she feels the only "safe" plan is to go back to him. This can then snowball for the victim, because when things go bad again and she looks to leave, where does she go? All her friends and family are upset with her and think she's crazy, just like he said. The support system unwittingly plays right into the hands of the abuser.

I've discussed some of these issues previously in this book but want to address them again. If you have a loved one or a good friend who is in an abusive relationship or has left one recently be supportive and patient. Don't be quick to judge, but listen and examine what that person has been through. Let them talk things out without being judged or ridiculed. You might think they sound a bit on the crazy side of things but that's OK, let them work it out. Validate and support and let them be themselves. I have found the best way is for them to work out their own issues without being told what to think or do or say. The results are very beneficial, especially for the survivor.

Dealing with the "System"

One of the worst nightmares for many clients is having to work with the legal and judicial system. This can be anything from being willing to testify if the DA brings charges against the partner for spousal abuse, to having to sit down with a family court mediator to decide custody issues.

The courts are obviously overcrowded, and the personnel are overworked. Judges hear complicated, confusing, and abusive stories all day. It is a constant stream of "he said, she said" cases. The advocates are there for help but they have no control over the court system or the judges' decisions. I know first-hand that the advocates working for the Marjaree Mason Center are excellent in the way they help the clients but they cannot protect the survivor from being blind-sided by a court decision that favors the abuser and slams the victim. This happens all too frequently, and unless survivors are aware of this possibility, they can be very devastated by it. Remember that the nature of the abusive relationship is that the abuser has all the power and oftentimes has all the money.

In family court, he can hire himself a good attorney while the victim/survivor has no funds for such things and might stand before the judge with no one representing her but herself. I've had so many clients who do hire attorneys but then the attorney seems helpless to do anything on her behalf and tells her to just accept whatever happens. She winds up accused of being responsible for all the problems. In disbelief she looks around, finds herself frustrated and angry, and shows her emotions. The court then looks at her and sees an angry woman and hears the abuser saying, "See what I have to deal with, Your Honor?" The victim then becomes re-victimized by the system she thought would protect her and be on her side.

In criminal court, it's the DA who brings charges against the abuser for spousal abuse and other charges. This doesn't mean the victim necessarily achieves any sense of satisfaction. Because the courts are overloaded and the jails and prisons are so overcrowded, the DA often offers plea deals that are sometimes astounding. I am familiar with a case in which the abuser assaulted his victim, raped her, and threatened her life. There was plenty of evidence to support the charges. However, the plea offer was no jail time and five years probation with the "threat" that if he did anything wrong during those five years, then he would go to prison for sure. He went on his way and did plenty wrong but was never called on by the probation officer or the courts and totally walked away from this incident with no consequences. I know the DA was doing her job, and I understand the need to expedite certain cases. However, I also know that one of the outcomes of this decision was that the victim's teenage son was so angered by this lack of judgment he decided he could do anything he wanted and figured there would be no consequences. He talked about killing the abuser and had the means to do it but his mother convinced him it wasn't a wise move. As of this writing, he is still heavily into drugs and alcohol and is verbally abusive to his partner. He must be responsible for his own actions, and I'm not saying it's the court's fault. But there are far-reaching consequences to their decisions and these are many times not favorable.

Call the Cops

Another area of great concern for victims/survivors is the idea of calling the police when an abuse incident occurs. I've had many, many clients tell me, "The cops don't do anything. They might take him away for a few hours but then they let him out and he comes right back. Then there is real hell to pay, and you think I'm gonna call the cops again? No way!"

It is a very difficult situation for law enforcement. I've ridden with police officers on domestic violence calls. I've heard one party say all that the partner did to them, and then I heard the partner say all the things the other person did to them. It is confusing, and both can be so believable. Officers receive extensive training in domestic violence calls but unless you are exposed to it every day, you really can't tell who's lying and who's telling the truth.

In some cases, both parties are exaggerating and the truth is somewhere in the middle of their stories. However, I've seen cases where the manipulative abuser has so set up the circumstances that the victim is arrested as being the abuser. This has happened many times to my clients. When it does, they are treated as abusers and are sentenced to batterer's treatment programs and anger management and family parenting classes, and the list goes on. They struggle with it but usually do what they are told. Meanwhile, the abuser is off partying and having a good time, laughing about the whole thing.

I had a client once who walked in on her husband and his friends doing drugs. She had accused him of doing drugs so many times, and every time he would become abusive and angry and leave the house. This time, when she walked in on it, he went ballistic. He beat her severely. She came to my office in crisis. A female co-therapist took pictures of all the bruises and injuries she suffered. The police were called and he was arrested for spousal abuse. However, the next day, he was released and no charges were filed. When she asked how they could do that, given her bruises and all the officers had seen, they replied that they had interviewed all the witnesses and they all agreed that she'd done it all to herself. They reported that she had thrown herself on the ground and done all the injuries to herself right in front of them. Mind you, the "witnesses" were his drug buddies, but that didn't matter. They were the witnesses, and that was the basis for letting him go with no charges filed. I haven't seen that client since her partner was released, so I wonder how things are going for her.

I've also had clients who tell of having officers show up to the scene and begin interrogating them. In these cases, the victim is challenged as to what she did to set him off, or they ask why she is still with this guy and ask what is wrong with her. The victim winds up totally re-victimized and feeling there is no help out there for her. What does she do the next time she needs help? Call the police for more abuse? Clients tend to say "no." There are definitely trust issues that develop in these cases. I try to discuss these situations with my clients and present possible answers or insights into why officers say what they say or do what they do or both. They are still the best option if the client is afraid for her life. As I've said before, the officers are in a most difficult place in dealing with domestic abuse situations. It is also, I've been told, one of the most dangerous calls an officer can be sent to. Many times, they arrived to re-establish peace in the situation and deal with the abuser, only to have the victim attack them to defend her abuser. Obviously, these are potentially very dangerous situations at times.

I must also say that I've had some clients tell me of quick, supportive action by officers arriving on the scene. One client was facing a very dangerous situation in which her abuser was preparing to kill her adult son, who had been ready to attack back. Officers arrived and immediately jumped into the scene, risking their own lives to protect her son. They moved quickly to calm the situation, arrested her abusive partner, and took statements from the client and her son. They were totally accepting of her plight and offered all the help they could at the time. Others have told such stories as well and have a high level of respect for officers. One client has experienced both in various incidents and stated her confusion one day in session: "I just don't know who is going to show up, good cop or bad cop."

My recommendation was that she consider getting out of the situation so she would never need to call the police.

Family Court Mediators

Believe it or not, this is the one situation in which I get the most complaints. Clients dealing with family court mediators find they are hurt and misunderstood so many times that in sessions with clients going into this process, I warn them to be prepared. Indeed, in one workshop with mediators, I was told that they receive extensive training in domestic violence. This may be true but at times it seems that I almost do more therapy with clients recovering from being victimized by mediators than being abused by abusers. I'm not saying that all mediators are bad. Indeed, I've had wonderful occasions when clients tell me how great their mediator was and how they clearly understood the situation the client was in. These have been awesome experiences, and I am grateful to those mediators who truly understand domestic abuse relationships. However, far more are the negative experiences.

One client went into mediation and requested they have separate meetings with the mediator. Her abuser was present, and she was totally intimidated by him. He stood six foot, seven inches and she was five foot, two inches. He was menacing and had "that" look in his eyes, according to the client. The mediator told her that there was a security guard right outside the door and she was safe. The client insisted it wasn't a fear of being attacked but just being in the same room with him and hearing his voice and feeling his presence. The mediator proceeded by saying that since they were both there already it would be senseless to delay by setting up separate meetings. They "proceeded," with the mediator listening intently to all the abuser had to say and cutting off the client whenever she wanted to say anything. When it was the client's turn to speak, the mediator kept allowing the abuser to interrupt. The more this went on, the more upset the client became. Eventually, the mediator asked her if she was upset. When the client tried to explain what was bothering her, the mediator responded by saying that the client obviously had an anger issue and needed to get some anger management classes. All the time, the abuser sat there calm and smiling. He was in total control. It took months to get the client back to a point of having any hope of getting on with her life.

Another client had her mediator offer her 50/50 custody of the couple's three children when she walked in the door. She hadn't even sat down yet. Her abusive partner wasn't there because he was sitting in jail facing attempted murder charges. The client pointed this out to the mediator and said she didn't think the 50/50 idea would work very well.

The stories go on and on. In defense of mediators, I know they face an incredibly difficult workload. Those of us who don't do that job have no idea how stressful it can be. They have hundreds of couples to work with and a very serious responsibility on their shoulders in making recommendations to the courts. Still, my understanding is that the policies and procedures call for separate sessions in domestic abuse cases if the party requests it. The mediators are trained in domestic violence but I wonder if they know how to recognize the smoothness of the abusive manipulator in their presence.

Stay Focused

My point here is to prepare the survivor, and those who care about her, for the potential difficulties in this arena. When they are facing such situations, I encourage clients to keep their focus on themselves and what they are there for. If they stay calm and focused, they are able to speak their minds, make their points, and experience some sense of success. Otherwise, they get emotional and their anger can get the best of them, and they make themselves easy targets for the abuser's manipulations.

Know your rights and demand them if necessary. So many abuse victims go into court acting like a victim and, in so doing, become victimized even more. You are no longer a victim but rather a survivor. Act like one. Know what you can do and what you can't, and be focused on you. The abuser can only intimidate you if you let him under your skin and into your mind. You then become externally focused and lose your concentration on why you are there. Take support with you if possible: family, friends, advocates, or whoever is available to support you. They may not be allowed to speak or even be given such an opportunity but they will be there for you to make eye contact with, and sometimes that makes all the difference.

Unless you are ready to do so, don't make eye contact with the abuser. The eyes are one of the sharpest weapons of control. The survivor knows all too well what the eyes of her abuser say and mean. One look is all it takes. I've had clients tell me of looking at him in court and his eyes say everything. She knows that if he could reach across the table or get to her seat, she'd be dead. It stirs such fear inside. What happens if they let him go? What happens when he gets out? Fear. Sometimes the abuser tells the victim that if he should ever go to jail or prison, then his buddies will take care of her. She knows what that means and lives daily in fear of the knock on the door or someone walking up to her or driving by her somewhere. Fear. This is one of the primary reasons that victims will recant or change their testimony when it comes time for trial. They fear the consequences of their actions. This is why it is such a brave and courageous thing for a victim to become a survivor and stand up for herself and make her statements before law enforcement and the courts.

To those who make it to this point and are getting away and then having to deal with the "system," I say stick it out. Find help in the form of a good advocate, a good therapist, perhaps a woman's shelter with a support staff such as the Marjaree Mason Center in Fresno. There are many across the country, and I've heard of some wonderful outcomes through their help. It's a rough road and a demanding task, with most of the power stacked against you. However, it can be done, and done successfully. I have many stories of clients who have met the challenge. Yes, there are those sessions filled with tears, as the client says it's too hard, there's no way to win. But they stick to it.

One client had no money to hire an attorney so she would go to court representing herself. Her husband was a disbarred attorney who had lots of attorney friends and knew most of the judges. Most of them were afraid of him because they knew what type of person he was. She was trying to get sole custody of her daughter, and despite the abuser's drug use and known participation in pornography and with prostitutes, he would win every time. Other attorneys would come up to her and tell her to give it up. Still, she persisted. After almost five years of struggle, she finally won and won big. She was awarded full custody and the right to remove the daughter from the county where they lived. She was ready and moved the next month.

Others have gone through tough trials and have had to testify in front of the abuser, his attorney, and his family all sitting and staring. Still they maintain their focus and make it through. Not all win their cases, and life takes on new twists and turns as they struggle to be free of the abuse and control. But they are survivors and they make it.

Survivor's Corner

"You're just trying to win a case. I'm fighting for my life here!"

Tammy, a survivor talking to
a public defender outside
the courtroom where he was
defending her abusive husband.

Chapter Fourteen

Safety Planning

It is my recommendation to those who are in abusive relationships that they need to do safety planning. Those who have friends or loved ones caught in these relationships need to be available as much as possible and in whatever ways are workable to assist in this plan. Below are some suggestions for effective safety planning.

Pack a Suitcase

Oftentimes, when an attack starts, the victim doesn't have time to pull out a suitcase and pack and prepare to leave. I've had clients tell me of trying to put things in a suitcase only to have the abuser take things out just as fast as she puts them in. He throws them around the room and, in one case, used the suitcase as a weapon to beat her. So they should pack a suitcase before such an attack occurs. Once the suitcase is packed, store it at a neighbor's or a relative's place. You want it somewhere you can get to it on a moment's notice after you leave the house.

What to pack? You want enough clothes for yourself, and the children if they go with you. We're talking socks, underwear, nightwear, diapers, toiletries, etc. You want enough for at least a few days. Also include other items such as copies of important documents including your driver's license; Social Security cards; birth certificates; children's school registration papers and/or immunizations records; prescriptions; medical histories; any legal documents such as restraining orders; tax returns; bank statements; credit card statements; address books; keepsakes important to you (this is important because I've had many clients leave the house only to come back and find he has destroyed everything he knew meant anything to her); copies of keys such as the house, car, and safe deposit box key; and others. Also put cash money in the suitcase. Put enough to live on for a while.

I know this is a task and not something you can do out in the open. Take your time. Plan this out. Hopefully, it will be something you never have to use, but you never know.

I say to pack a suitcase but sometimes that can be too obvious. I had a client who used garbage bags. The house was a mess because he kept pulling the drawers out of the dressers and searching through them for signs she was having an affair. She got tired of putting everything back so she reached a point of just leaving things lying around and the drawers open and empty. When she was told about the need to plan and prepare to leave when the opportunity presented itself, she grabbed garbage bags and started putting clothes and other things in them. One bag was for her, one for her young son, and one for her even younger daughter. She put things in the bags and then tossed them into a corner of the room. One day, after her abusive partner had been up for three days and abusing her constantly, she'd had enough. He went to bed and fell asleep. She got the kids and gave each one their bag, and they crept towards the front door. She sent her son to the car first. Before she could get herself and her daughter out of the house, though, he woke up. She said they froze at the front door while he walked down the hall to the bathroom. As he came back, she said they just stood by the door. If he had turned to the left, he would have walked into the living room and seen them. If he had turned to the right, then he'd head back into the bedroom and go to sleep. It seemed like an eternity, she said, but he turned to the right. She waited for a few minutes, and then they slipped out the door and to the car. She went to a shelter and stayed for a week or so until he found her. She moved again and he found her again. When I saw her, she was on her sixth move, and as far as she knew, he hadn't found her for the last two. Still, we worked together for a few months, and then she was suddenly gone. My heart goes out to her and her children, and I hope they are OK.

The idea here is to think outside the box. Be creative in your planning.

Document the Abuse

Keep a hidden journal and write down dates and times and what happened. In your writing, also put down quotes of things said. Get photos taken if possible and keep them stashed. Polaroid photos are sufficient. Just something to document that the abuse happened. Show your injuries to a friend or a relative so that others witness the bruises or scrapes. Be sure this is a friend you can count on and trust. If you can, make copies of bills for repairs to damaged doors or walls or other household items. All of this is evidence for the court. Things such as pictures and written documents with dates and times are what the court needs to truly understand what's happened. Otherwise, it's "he said, she said," and the courts will throw it all out.

Prepare Yourself within the House

Be aware of your surroundings within the house. If physical abuse is occurring, you need to know your escape routes. Put yourself in any given room in the house and imagine yourself being attacked. How do you get out of that room? Through a door? Out the window? Know where your phones are and have a cell phone with you. Remember, if you need to call 911 and you use your house phone, you don't need to talk to the dispatcher who answers. Your address will come up on the dispatcher's screen. If you call and can talk, then do so, but if you can't, make the call and put the phone down and start screaming. The dispatcher will hear you and send help. However, if you are using your cell phone, no address will come up on the dispatcher's screen. You need to stay on the phone in that case to give your address and describe the situation. Remove all weapons from the house if possible. Know where you would go if you had to on a moment's notice.

Code Words

I encourage people to develop code words with friends or relatives and also with the children. This can be anything that works for you. The purpose is that if you need to call for help, sometimes he won't let you make a call because he thinks you're calling the police. In those cases, don't call the police but rather call your friend or relative with whom you have set this code word. If you can call them, use the code word and then finish the conversation. The friend or relative knows that by you using the code, they need to call the police for you and also to come over to your house if possible.

I had a client once who had done this with a good friend of hers. The code word was "pumpkin pie." One night, her abuser was basically chasing her around the house and beating her. This had gone on for some time, and he finally sat down. She went to the phone and began dialing. He jumped to his feet and came and accused her of calling 911.

She said, "No, I'm calling Susie."

"I'm gonna stand right here and listen," he said. "If I hear the cops, then you're dead!"

Well, she called Susie and asked how she was doing and tried to be as nonchalant as possible. In the course of the short conversation, however, she asked, "Susie, do you still have that pumpkin pie recipe we talked about? I'd love to make one, and if you could get it to me, I'd sure appreciate it."

"The pumpkin pie recipe?" Susie asked to make sure she'd heard her right.

"Yes, the pumpkin pie recipe we talked about."

"OK, sure, I'll find it and get it to you tomorrow or so," was Susie's reply.

With that, my client hung up the phone. It didn't keep him from starting up his attack on her again. But shortly afterwards, she ran out of the house with him in pursuit with a hammer in his hand. As they emerged from the house and into the front yard, he came face to face with several police officers who had just pulled up. And there was Susie and her husband, who was a retired officer himself.

Another client set up a codeword with her landlord. She had told her about how abusive her live-in boyfriend was and that she needed help. The landlord agreed to the use of the codeword "cheesecake" and they devised a safety plan together. About a month later the landlord got a text message late one night from my client. It consisted of one word – "cheesecake". That was all she was able to get out before he yanked the phone from her hands and broke it. The landlord called the police who showed up at the door just as my client's abusive boyfriend was breaking in the bathroom door where she had locked herself away for protection from his physical attack.

The idea of code words for the children has to do with the need to get the kids out of the house quickly. One client established a code word with her children and had to use it one night. She had come home from work and was "five minutes late." When she walked into the house, she couldn't find her husband. She asked the kids where he was and was told he was in the garage. She walked out into a dark garage and found him sitting in a chair.

"You're late! Were you out with that guy?" he asked.

"No, I just got home and it's only five minutes later than usual."

"How long have you been seeing him? I know you were with him!" he barked.

My client knew what she was in store for that night, and something clicked inside. "I can't do this anymore," she remembered saying to herself.

"Tell you what," she said, "let me get the kids settled with some dinner and then we can talk."

"OK," was his reply.

She walked back into the house and called out to the kids, "Hey, guys, let's go get some anchovy pizza!" That was the code word phrase she had set up with them. The kids knew that meant to grab a little bag each had put in their room, and they went straight to the car. Within a couple of minutes, she was driving away from the house and did not return until weeks later, when she went with police officers to get the rest of her things.

I'm not sure why most people use food words for code words, but if it works, hey, great! Code words can work miracles. Set them up.

Find a Shelter or Other Safe Place

In the course of your day, find the location of a shelter or line up a place with friends or relatives. Establish someplace you can go to on a moment's notice and be safe. The lady I mentioned above who snuck out of the house with her two kids as her abusive husband went back to sleep, made her move only after she had discovered there was a woman's shelter in her town. Until then, she hadn't known there was such a place and fairly close. Once she knew and had it lined up, it was just a matter of time.

When You Leave

Leaving may be the hardest thing in the world to do. Try to leave while your partner is away or asleep, or call and ask the police to be present to "keep the peace" while you leave. They will come but they won't stay long so you have to be prepared to move quickly. Protect yourself first. If you cannot take the children with you, don't assume you will lose custody. Leaving because you fear for your life or safety is perfectly legitimate in the eyes of law enforcement and the courts. Get legal assistance as quickly as possible. This doesn't necessarily mean you have to get an attorney, but you do need to meet with a paralegal or find an agency that will offer you legal support. Try to line this up before you leave if possible. If you leave your children behind and are fearful they might be hurt, call Child Protective Services or the police as soon as possible.

Remember, when a victim leaves is the most dangerous time in the whole relationship. Be vigilant but not paranoid. Be observant and aware of your surroundings. Rely on your support system if you have one. If you don't, develop one as best you can.

Chapter Fifteen

Success Stories

I believe I've put out a lot of information in this book. It's a lot for a person to take in and digest. I know in groups I've presented to, as well as classes I've taught, it can be a bit overwhelming and even discouraging. Looking into the world of domestic abuse, looking behind the bruises into the world of psychological, emotional, and verbal abuse can be disturbing at best.

As I've mentioned earlier in this text, I think getting out of an abusive relationship might be one of the hardest things a person can do. It's facing thoughts of failure, feelings of loss; there are major shifts in reality, if you will. It is also reclaiming self with all the hopes and dreams and goals that the victim had prior to being abused. It's a time of rekindling the belief that life can be good, and even more, that a relationship can be good.

In this chapter, I felt it was important to share some success stories of those who have gotten out and changed their lives around. I've mentioned some in other chapters but wanted to bring them together here as a notice of support that the "victim" can change herself, or himself, into a "survivor" or even a "thriver," as some have called themselves. There is hope, and a lot of very hard work, at the end of an abusive relationship. There is life out there!

One lady, about twenty-five or so, used to come into sessions dressed in sweats and with her hair pulled back tight against her head. She would sit in the chair during sessions, with her body slumped to one side and looking down most of the time. Her abuser had attempted to kill her and was caught in the act by police. He was going off to prison, and she was trying to get on with her life. She was confused, scared, and in pain. We worked together for almost a year when she got an opportunity to go work in another town, a few hours' driving time away. We discussed the move because she wanted to do it but was terrified of leaving Fresno, as she'd never been away from her home and her parents.

Eventually, she took the job and moved away but we stayed in touch by phone every week for the next several months. Then it got to where we'd talk about every other month. Then, after a year or so, she indicated she'd gotten another job offer in a town at the opposite end of the state. She was being recognized for her great work and felt the promotion was an opportunity she couldn't pass up.

As such things go, we lost touch, and I often thought about her and wondered what she was doing. Then one day, I was walking through an office complex here in Fresno when suddenly I heard, "Bob???"

I turned and there she was. Standing all of her six feet in height, dressed in a smart-looking business suit, hair all full and hanging down to her shoulders; she smiled and gave me the biggest hug.

"How have you been?" we both asked at the same time.

She informed me that she was back in Fresno at a new job and that she was making six figures! She looked great and told me she felt great. I asked her if she was dating anyone or was with anyone.

Her reply made me laugh: "Why would I want to share any of this with a man?"

She did say she was thinking about dating but hadn't done any yet. She then quickly added that if she did start seeing a man, that he'd have to be healthy and that she was well aware of the "red flags" we had talked about years before. We've run into each other a few times since then, and she continues to thrive. Another client of mine went through so much trial and tribulation trying to get away from her abuser. He was a master manipulator and very intelligent. He would twist statements she made and was constantly trying to get her into court to use the system against her. It seemed he had endless amounts of money to keep attorneys busy on her case while she struggled to get through school and have the chance to get a job in her career field.

The main source of contention was their three children. He had neglected them constantly when they were a family together. Now he claimed he was the only loving parent and that she was neglectful of the kids while she went to school. She struggled for over a year, dealing with all the mediation and re-victimization as her abuser manipulated the situation. So many times she would break down in sessions and cry and wonder if she would have been better off just staying in the abuse.

Then one day, in court, her ex-husband/abuser made a statement that the judge objected to. Suddenly, the abuser was angry and showed his temper to the court. No matter what his attorney could do, the man was enraged and showed what he was really like.

My client took great joy in telling the judge, "You see what I've had to live with, Your Honor?"

Everything changed that day. She described it as if the clouds broke open and the sun shown through. She was awarded custody of the children and given permission to move, with the kids, to another city where she'd gotten a job offer in her chosen career. Today, she is a single mom, living a happy life with the kids. She's happy in her job and making a great living. Yes, the children see their dad in supervised visitation. My client is now happy she stuck with it and persevered to the end of all the court battles, despite all the hard times she had to go through.

A gentleman I have worked with fits the category of "success story" for sure. When we started, the relationship he was in was best described as mutually combative. Both partners would get to a point they'd say things and act out with each other in very abusive ways. It wasn't always physical, but the verbal abuse was intense. He came to me asking for help, saying he hated these episodes and that it wasn't the way he wanted things to be at all. What was compounding the situation was that they had a small child together. This little girl was being exposed to all this violence, and the father felt so bad for her.

"How do I change?" he asked. "How do I make things right?"

Notice he wasn't asking how could he change his partner. He wasn't asking how could he learn to cope with her when she pushed his buttons. He wasn't accusing her of anything at all. He would question why she did certain things or acted certain ways, but there was never any accusations. This impressed me, and I knew that if he stayed with it, he could change himself, and as for the relationship, well, we'd just have to see where that went.

He worked hard on his own issues. He learned how to communicate in healthy ways and tried to implement those qualities into his discussions with his partner. Despite his efforts, it didn't work. She always seemed intent on creating as much drama as possible. One of the worst times was one night when she was using every trick in the book to get him upset. She even resorted to calling his mom all sorts of names. He stayed calm. He expressed being upset that she would talk that way, but he refused to engage in arguing. The calmer he was, the more irate she became. Finally, in a fit of rage, she broke some things and stormed out of the house. It was his house, and the next day, while she was still away, he changed the locks. When she came back a couple of days later, he told her she could get her things and that he would help her move but she had to leave. He was calling it quits. She moved out and got her own place.

Today they exchange their daughter amicably and are agreeable enough with each other. What impresses me is that he has continued to work on himself. He attends counseling regularly and works on his communications skills, his boundary settings, and learning about himself. He's worked on family-of-origin issues and setting goals for himself. He has learned to recognize controlling behavior, whether in himself or others, and has vowed to teach his daughter how to treat people right, with respect, and to expect others to treat her the same way. I can't find a better representative of "success."

There are many more success stories. The journeys have been very difficult but these people have made the steps necessary to get free of the abuse and begin their own lives again. Each of those I've mentioned, and others, have told me how they now look for opportunities to help others get free. The success stories continue.

Survivor's Corner

"Whatever!"

This became the slogan of a support group of women survivors of domestic violence I used to facilitate. They were tired of dealing with mental and verbal manipulations by their abusive partners. It became their response to every explanation, every excuse, and every attempt to engage them in an argument. For them, it worked!

A Final Note

I have put this collection of information and observations together in an attempt to help as many victims of abusive relationships as I can. It is my hope that anyone who reads through it can get a glimpse of what victims/survivors are going through. You cannot "feel what they feel" unless you yourself have been there. But you can understand and support those caught in such a "crazy-making" world, whether they be a man or a woman.

To families and relatives and friends who read this information, continue to love the one caught in the trap of abuse. Love, listen, and be ready to help when the call comes … and hope for that call. I know you probably don't understand why they stay or what they are thinking. The abuser may try to sway you to believe your loved one is mad at you or blames you. At the very least, the abuser makes it out that it's all the victim's fault. Stand by your loved one or friend. It might be very frustrating for you, and even scary. Hold on to your hope for them and be patient.

It is never my place to tell anyone to leave a relationship. It's not my call, nor is it yours. It is up to the one caught up in that abusive cycle.

To victims, I can only admire your persistence and the strength of your love and devotion. However, your love and devotion cannot change the abuser. You are entitled to your dream of a happy family, but it will not happen with an abuser. Can such an abuser change?

Yes! But it won't be successful if it's done for you or for the family. The abuser must change for the abuser's own sake. You must change for your own sake.

If you are in the midst of an abusive relationship — please get help in any way you can. There are those people out there who do understand and who offer support. Some are survivors themselves who have been through what you are going through. Reach out — there is help available. You too can be a survivor and, in turn, help others. One by one, we take the steps together to stop domestic violence.

Survivor's Corner

"Before, I always left because I
was hurt.

This time, I'm leaving because I'm
finished!"

Miriam

About the Author

Bob Meade, MA, LMFT is a licensed Marriage and Family Therapist who has been in the domestic violence field for many years, working as a counselor, group facilitator, and teacher. During this time, he has spent thousands of hours with hundreds of people caught in the web of abuse: women, men, and children; victims and perpetrators.

Over the years, Bob has developed his practical, down-to-earth style of teaching and therapy through the many paths life has taken him. Bob has worked several careers and many, many jobs in a wide variety of fields. He has learned a little about life from being an elementary school teacher, ordained non-denominational minister, librarian, bank teller, television show producer, and door-to-door salesman as well as laboring in a rock quarry, planting trees in the forests of Oregon and Washington, roofing, as a factory laborer, and even driving an ice cream truck. Throughout it all, he has sought to learn lessons and grow, gaining insights he now shares with those he counsels and teaches.

Bob was featured in an episode of *Anatomy of Crime* on the Court TV national cable network. His fifteen seconds of fame was part of a segment featuring one of his clients, a true survivor, who has overcome a horribly abusive relationship that featured extreme mental, emotional, verbal, and physical abuse that included guns.

He also teaches workshops on domestic violence at local colleges and is recognized as an expert witness in domestic violence issues by the Fresno County Superior Court system.

A great believer in object lessons, movie lines, and other quotes, Bob uses everyday life to make his material relevant and practical. Having suffered through abuse of various types as a child and as an adult, Bob can empathize with those dealing with abuse issues today. As a "success story" himself, he looks to help others succeed in their lives.

Bob was prompted to write this book as a practical guide for those seeking to understand the world of domestic violence. Family, friends, and clients have encouraged production of this work for those caught up in abuse as well as the victim/survivor's family and friends. He now makes it available for anyone seeking to learn about this crazy-making world of abusive relationships.

If the reader would like to contact the author about what this book has meant to them or wishes to share their own stories, please contact him at: spincyclestop@yahoo.com

Lightning Source UK Ltd.
Milton Keynes UK
12 January 2010

148489UK00001BB/261/P